The Minimalist Lifestyle 101

The road map to declutter your life and save money with a minimalist lifestyle

© **Copyright 2019 –Julia Valente All rights reserved.**

ISBN 978-0-6486577-2-9

The content contained within this book may not be reproduced, duplicated or transmitted without direct written permission from the author or the publisher.

Under no circumstances will any blame or legal responsibility be held against the publisher, or author, for any damages, reparation, or monetary loss due to the information contained within this book. Either directly or indirectly.

Legal Notice:

This book is copyright protected. This book is only for personal use. You cannot amend, distribute, sell, use, quote or paraphrase any part, or the content within this book, without the consent of the author or publisher.

Disclaimer Notice:

Please note the information contained within this document is for educational and entertainment purposes only. All effort has been executed to present accurate, up to date, and reliable, complete information. No warranties of any kind are declared or implied. Readers acknowledge that the author is not engaging in the rendering of legal, financial, medical or professional advice. The content within this book has been derived from various sources. Please consult a licensed professional before attempting any techniques outlined in this book.

By reading this document, the reader agrees that under no circumstances is the author responsible for any losses, direct or indirect, which are incurred as a result of the use of information contained within this document, including, but not limited to, — errors, omissions, or inaccuracies.

Table Of Contents

Introduction 1
Chapter One: Introduction To Minimalism 2
Chapter Two: Why People Strive Towards Being A Minimalist 6
   Benefits Of Minimalism.. 6
      Contentment 6
      Save Time 7
      Freedom 7
      Better Health 7
      Personal Growth... 7
      Cleaner Home.. 7
      Aids In Success... 8
      Save Money 8
      Encourages A Giving Nature... 8
      Set An Example 8
      Environmental Consciousness... 9
      Aesthetic Appeal.. 9
Chapter Three: How To Live A Minimalist Lifestyle? 10
   Focus On Family And Loved Ones 10
   Get Rid Of Unnecessary Possessions 11
   Get A Job That You Love 11
   Spend Your Time Well 12
   Practice Self-Care.. 12
   Appreciate Your Present... 13
   Stay Strong During The Bad Times 13
   Stop Chasing Happiness 14
Chapter Four: The Minimalist Budget 15
   50/30/20 Rule... 19

Chapter Five: Tips On How To Create A Minimalist Closet 21

   Be Selective 21

   Individual Style 22

   Focus On Quality And Not Quantity 22

   Ignore The Latest Trends 23

   Experiment 24

   Stick To Your Budget 24

   Segregate Clothes 25

   Tips To Declutter Your Closet 25

      Take Everything Out Of Your Closet First 25

      Think Well About The Clothes You Decide To Keep 25

      Give Away Or Sell 26

      Bags And Shoes 26

      Accessories 27

      Organize 27

Chapter Six: Minimalist Wardrobe 30

   Stylist Wendy Mak Rule Of 30 Clothes 30

      Bottoms 32

      Tops 33

      Dresses 33

      Jackets 33

      Bags 34

      Shoes 34

Chapter Seven: Tips On How To Create A Minimalist Living Room 36

   Tips To Declutter Your Living Room: 37

Chapter Eight: How To Setup A Minimalist Kitchen – Things To Avoid 40

    Things To Avoid In A Minimalist Kitchen 40

Chapter Nine: How To Set Up A Minimalist Bathroom .. 46

Chapter Ten: How To Set Up A Minimalist Bedroom 49

    Make Your Bed.. 49

    Revamp Your Wardrobe And Drawers.. 50

    Organize Your Desk 51

    Clear The Bedside Table 52

    Get Rid Of Unwanted Accessories.. 53

    Throw Out Old Unused Beauty Products................................... 53

    Get Rid Of Unwanted Furniture... 53

    Get Rid Of Unwanted Shoes 54

Chapter Eleven: Tips On How To Set Up A Minimalist Office 55

    Arrange The Books 56

    Check Old And Unwanted Files... 56

    Collect Miscellaneous 56

    Decluttering Drawers 57

    Clean Out Shelves 57

    Clean Out Your Personal Desktop... 58

    Do Not Forget To Declutter Your Walls 59

Chapter Twelve: Declutter For Minimalist 61

    17 Simple Tips To Declutter Your Home................................... 61

    What You Need 61

    The Throw Bag.. 62

    The Recycling Bag... 62

    The Donate Bag... 62

    The Sell Bag 62

    Declutter Tip Number 1 – Repack A Room............................... 62

- Declutter Tip Number 2 – Play With Numbers 63
- Declutter Tip Number 3 – Make Micro-Lists 63
- Declutter Tip Number 4 – Set A Timer 63
- Declutter Tip Number 5 – Organise A Swap Party 64
- Declutter Tip Number 6 – Discard Broken Items...................... 64
- Declutter Tip Number 7 – Donate Books And Magazines To Hospital Emergency Rooms 65
- Declutter Tip Number 8 – Roll Your T-Shirts 65
- Declutter Tip Number 9 – Cut Down Your Towel Rotation 65
- Declutter Tip Number 10 – Organise Before You Buy................. 65
- Declutter Tip Number 11 – Be Realistic In Your Vision 66
- Declutter Tip Number 12 – Designate A Spot For Incoming Paper 66
- Declutter Tip Number 13 – Scan Your Paperwork 66
- Declutter Tip Number 14 – Sort By Categories, Not By Room.... 67
- Declutter Tip Number 15 – Define Your Why Statement 67
- Declutter Tip Number 16 – Chronicle Your Journey.................. 68

Chapter Thirteen: The Minimalist Approach, Clear That Clutter 69
- Tips And Ideas To Create The Minimalist Look 69

Chapter Fourteen: Living In A Tiny Home 71
- The Benefits Of Living In A Tiny Home: 72
- Tips For Building And Maintaining A Tiny Home......................75
- How To Keep A Tiny Home Decluttered:......................................78
  - One In, One Out Rule..78
- Fixed Number Of Possessions 78
- Assign Areas..78
- Storage Bins 79
- Use And Give Away...79

Chapter Fourteen: Challenges In Minimalism And How To Overcome Them 80

Chapter Fifteen: Being A Minimalist On A Holiday 86

Chapter Sixteen: How To Practice Minimalism With Your Smartphone 90

Physical And Mental Overhaul 94

Conclusion 99

Reference 100

Introduction

I want to thank you for choosing this book, *'Minimalism - How to simplify your life and live with less'* and hope you find the book informative and interesting.

Most human beings are extremely emotional and out of these emotions, we tend to accumulate a lot of things under the name of nostalgia. In reality, it is nothing but clutter. As much as we all would like to deny it, most of us are hoarders of petty things that have or at one point in time had any emotional value. I for one have a lot of old movie tickets from dates, boarding passes for flights, jewelry and trinkets that I had as a kid and other such things that have no actual value in my life at the present.

Then came a time in my life I looked back at the things I have hoarded over the years and decided that enough is enough. I had to take control of my life and turn things around and that is when I turned to minimalism. The concept of minimalism is less is more and living in the present and that is exactly what I have decided to live by.

Since I turned a minimalist, my life has become simple, clutter free and happy. The reason I started writing this book is because I want to share the secret of my happy and sorted life with everyone and help them lead a content life. In the course of this book, I have shared practical tips on how to live as a minimalist. If you follow these tips and make a conscious effort to bring about a change in your life, you will see a sea of change in your lifestyle for the best. Your life will be happier, improved and you will also save a lot of money in the bargain. So what are you waiting for? Let us read on and learn about minimalism in every walk of life and make life better.

Thank you once again for choosing this book. Good luck!

Chapter One
Introduction to Minimalism

Living a minimalist life has different concepts to many people. If I can ask, does it mean that you have to lack something in order to live minimally? Minimalism begins in the mind; it is about owning manageable items; however, it goes past more than just 'items.' It goes beyond health, wealth and even relationships.

A car is only meant to carry people to different destinations, but having 5 cars in the parking lot means just the same thing. Having one car may not only save fuel but also provide a quick decision that you can still use it the next day. But having 5 cars in your parking lot will clutter your mind and leave you having to make a decision every single time you drive which isn't necessary. You can't instantly decide which car that you are going to use. Furthermore, the vehicles would still continue to depreciate as far as they continue to remain in the parking lot. Why don't you just buy a decent car and save yourself from all these complications? It is not about enjoying life because you are able to, but it is about how you are loading your life with too much complication. Complications cause you to have stress but living a minimalist lifestyle is stress-free.

So what exactly is minimalism and who is considered a minimalist? Minimalism can mean something different to every individual. The main idea is to live a life that is more fulfilling and has a minimum number of possessions or distractions. Minimalism will help you to turn your focus towards things that are important and can provide you with long-term happiness. The world we live in today has turned our society towards materialism in a very unhealthy way.

People have started thinking of happiness in terms of the things they possess. There seems to be a limit to where we are allowed to be happy if we don't possess certain things. You cannot keep telling yourself that you will be successful and happy only when you own that expensive car or a huge mansion. Why can you not be happy without them? With the help of minimalism, you can. There is no exact definition of minimalistic living. People have different needs and wants so different things will be important to each person. The point is to focus on what is truly meaningful in your life and not place too much importance on what is not. The concept of minimalism should not scare you off. You don't have to sell off your car or shift to a tiny house to prove you are a minimalist. Some people choose to take these drastic steps, but there are others who are still considered minimalist even when they own certain possessions.

Minimalism will help you make positive changes in your life and more importantly, in your mindset. The mindset of an individual is what will make them minimalist and much happier than ever before. You have to understand that owning high-end shoes or clothes will not make you truly happy. When you buy one thing, there will always be something better to chase not long after. Materialism is an unending cycle that will never allow you to be satisfied with what you have. It has become a habit for people to want what they see someone else have. This is an unhealthy attitude that affects your health and growth. You can always work harder to strive for success in life but don't allow your position at a company or your possessions to define when you can be happy. Learning to be satisfied and grateful for what you already have is very important. You need to fight the current norms that society follows and think for yourself. There should not be any compulsion to follow the latest trends or buy the most expensive car to prove you are better than others. You need to make decisions for yourself and improve the way you live for your happiness.

When it comes to possessions, there is no fixed limit on how many you can have. You may have heard some people say that you should only have 100 material possessions in your house to be considered a minimalist. This is not true even if they choose to follow that limit. It is always better to own as little as possible, but you don't necessarily have to throw out what you want just to fit the label. Certain ideas surround minimalism because of the way minimalists portray themselves. You may choose to live like a minimalist who has no furniture in their room, but you will still be considered a minimalist if you decide to keep any furniture you want as well.

Minimalism will have a different significance for everyone. It is important to stop hoarding things over the years. Most people have the habit of keeping every single thing they spent money on or holding on to things that have sentimental value. You need to reduce the amount of importance you place on these things. What you possess or own will not define you. You have to start thinking about what is important to you and what you can afford to remove from your life. Think about what bothers you and stops you from living a truly fulfilling life. Get rid of those things. You don't have to quit your job if you can't afford to, try creating a better balance between your work and personal life instead. You may have a ton of things in your apartment, but the space is too little to accommodate everything well. Don't you think you would be able to stop complaining about your small apartment if you just got rid of the clutter that is taking up space there? This book will help you in improving your home and getting rid of clutter, regardless of how small or big the space is. Decluttering your space will be one of the best ways to start your transition to minimalism. You will be surprised by how many things have just been lying unused for years and how much more space you will have when you get rid of them. Don't stress about wasting the things that you feel are in good condition. You will be able to re-sell, donate or gift certain things to people less fortunate while the damaged items can be thrown away or recycled.

It is not just about how many things you own or want to own. A minimalist learns to differentiate between the things that matter and the things that don't. There is no right or a fixed way to be a minimalist. You have to understand that materialism can be a limitation on your happiness. Minimalism helps you to get rid of unnecessary things to make room for things in your life that are more fulfilling. You will learn how to be more mindful and make conscious decisions. Your actions have to be purposeful and so should your life. You don't have to be unhappy and work hard for years till you retire. Minimalism will help you become happier in your present and stay that way constantly through the years ahead. Your mind will be stress-free, and your mental health will take a turn for the better.

More importantly, you will see the positive impact it has on your relationships with family and friends. You need to make time for the people who matter in your life. They are the ones who will stand by you and support you even when things get hard. Don't alienate yourself to lead the ideal modern life that people work for these days. This book will help you take certain steps that will help you to craft a simpler and yet more fulfilling life for yourself. Minimalism will help you to be happy and content with all that you already have and assist in your efforts to reach any goals you have set for yourself. So keep reading and utilize this guide for a better life.

Chapter Two
Why People Strive towards Being a Minimalist

It is unfortunate that many people strive towards being a minimalist when they actually don't know what a minimalist life really entails. For some, minimalist living means living in a desolate state, and yet for others, it means luxurious living.

Other than having a lot of stuff, many people lack contentment. Wanting to get quick success won't guarantee the much-needed happiness; rather it will continue to make your life even more difficult. Minimalist living involves having enough for that period as long as the basic needs are met. Many people find it hard to be content possibly because they usually compete with other people. Don't sacrifice your sweet life to those material possessions that everyone out there is chasing.

There are scores of people out there who think that minimalist living is only meant for the loser class of society. For example, many people in the USA strive to win the lottery and some actually win, all in the hope of living happier lives. In my opinion, this is what society has made us believe. Ever heard of the saying "education is the key to success?" That is why a number of people are striving to get their children to school in the hope that they will get better lives and possibly help them in future.

Benefits of Minimalism

If you need further convincing to try implementing minimalism in your life, these following benefits will help you.

Contentment

It will help you become more content with everything that you have already been blessed with in your life. People lead an unhappy life when they place too much importance on material possessions and keep working to acquire these things. This discontentment prevents them from leading a happy life at any point no matter what.

Save time

Minimalism will help you save a lot of time in many different ways. You need to appreciate how precious your time is and stop wasting it on unnecessary things. The time you save can be used to do what you really enjoy or to invest in more productive matters. It will also help you in dedicating more time to your friends and family.

Freedom

Leading a minimalistic life will help you to gain freedom in certain ways. You will be free from any stress or fear that has resulted from your material life. You will also be free to pursue what you really want from your life.

Better health

A materialistic and unhealthy lifestyle inevitably has a negative impact on your health. Minimalism will help you to focus on improving your health so that you can lead a longer and better life.

Personal growth

Every person needs to make an effort to see some personal growth. Minimalism will help you to make mindful decisions and become more conscientious in your actions as well. You will grow to become a much better person and see improvement in various traits of your personality compared to before.

Cleaner home

Your home is the most important space in your life. Minimalism will help you declutter any mess, get rid of the excess and organize it in a much better way. It makes it much easier to maintain a clean and tidy home. A house with tons of things can be very hard to manage or clean. This can add stress and anxiety but it doesn't need to be this way.

Aids in success

Minimalism helps you to save time and energy that can be dedicated to achieving any goals you have. Your milestones for success will no longer be material possessions, and this will give you a clear perspective on what you should really aim for.

Save money

Materialism is the easiest way to burn off all the hard earned money that you have. Living minimally will teach you what you should really be spending your money on and how you can save money otherwise. When you save money, you will have more for investing and spending on what is really important or necessary. This can possibly lead to an early retirement if that's something that appeals to you.

Encourages a giving nature

The process of decluttering will help you to get rid of all the unnecessary things that have accumulated in your home over the years. Instead of throwing them away, you can donate them to the needy or just anyone who can find a better use for those things. Specifically, when it comes to things that have sentimental value for you, it is easier to give them to someone who will genuinely appreciate them as you did.

Set an example

If you want your children to learn from your mistakes and lead a better life, you need to set an example. Seeing you lead a minimalistic life will encourage them to do so as well. They will see and follow your ways of living as they grow up, they will learn to appreciate what they have and appreciate the value of money and relationships so it is essential to set a good example.

Environmental consciousness

Minimalism also encourages and teaches environmental consciousness. The materialistic culture has led to the production and waste of too much already. It has negatively impacted the environment and even contributed to climate change. As you learn to live with less, you will also waste less.

Aesthetic appeal

Minimalistic living is one of the most aesthetically pleasing ways to live. Your home and other spaces will have a cleaner and more effective design. Your own personal style will evolve in a better way as well. It will also be easier to maintain in the long term.

It is quite obvious by now that minimalism will only be beneficial for your life. There are so many different ways in which this lifestyle and mindset will positively impact your life. All these reasons and much more is why I seriously want to encourage you to have a go at this way of life. You might be a little doubtful at first, but these thoughts will wash away when you experience it for yourself. It will save you time, money and energy that are usually wasted on unnecessary things. Your mindset will switch to a much healthier one and help you live more happily as well and life is short so why wouldn't you want to cut out the negativity and replace them with positive vibes. The transition to minimalism is something you will never regret.

Chapter Three
How to Live a Minimalist Lifestyle?

You should have a general understanding of what minimalism is by now. Striving to live a minimalist life may seem daunting at first. Very few people are comfortable with the idea of letting go of their possessions. After all, haven't they worked most of their lives to get them in the first place? However, have those possessions or the current lifestyle you lead, given you real happiness? You may feel happy and satisfied at that very moment you buy something but the next day, there will be another thing that you want just as bad. This is why you need to find a way to live better and become truly happy in your life. You need to learn how to achieve peace of mind in the healthiest way possible.

Focus on Family and Loved Ones

It is very important that you understand who and what is really important in your life. Family and loved ones should be at the top of your priority list, not making sure you own the laters iPhone. Don't get so caught up in work and the chase of the modern world that you lose sight of these things. No matter how motivated you are to work hard and become successful, will it matter if you have no one to share the success with? A lot of people sacrifice their relationships for meaningless goals. Many people start paying unwarranted attention to people who will further their financial goals and compromise on their real relationships. Your time and effort have to be divided in a healthy way. These are the people who will support and stand by you when things get rough. You have to find a healthy work-life balance so that they get the time and attention they deserve. After all tomorrow is never guaranteed, we don't know how long we have on in this world so make time for those important people.

Get Rid of Unnecessary Possessions

Materialism is an enemy you need to defeat. Since you were young, you have probably been taught and shown that possessions are very important in life. This is one of the major drawbacks of this generation. Our ancestors definitely knew how to be happier with less; however, these days, everyone wants more and as much as they can possibly get. The chase for more material possessions seems never-ending. It might not seem like it but these possessions can be a real burden at times. They take up a lot of time and effort which can instead be invested for better purposes like education or learning a new skill. Materialism distracts you from the things which truly matter in your life. I'm not saying that you aren't minimalist if you own an iPad but basically you just have to start getting rid of the excess stuff you don't use and you can deny it all you want but don't need 20 pairs of shoes in your closet. You need to be able to differentiate what is important from what is not. Just because the market is growing, you don't have to buy the latest model of every new gadget that comes out. You may have more options, but you need to make better choices. Big companies will benefit from this culture, not you. Keep only what makes you happy in the long run.

Get a Job that You Love

It may seem idealistic but getting a job that you love is very important. You should at least like what you do, especially if you spend more than half your day at it. I had a job I absolutely hated for many years and even though it paid well, it took so much out of me mentally. I would leave work physically each day but mentally I couldn't switch off from it. It caused stress, anxiety and at the end of it all I wasn't able to save up anymore cash with the high paycheck I was getting every week because the more I earn, the more I spent. You may be really pressed for money, but when you live a more simplified life, your needs reduce and thus so does the amount of money you need. If you find a job you are good at or passionate about, you are more likely to excel at it. Anything worth doing is worth doing well. Don't stress yourself out at a job that does not provide any satisfaction in your life. If you don't have a financial pillow to fall back on, work for a while and save money. Then quit and find what you can do better. If you like your current job, you can still improve certain things within that job to improve your work life and satisfaction that you get from it.

Spend Your Time Well

Time is a commodity that is limited and as each minute, hour and day that we can't get back, we lose another opportunity to get the absolute most from our lives and be the best version of ourselves possible. Don't waste time on anything that does not make you happy or at peace. These things do not deserve any of your energy or attention. If you don't want to do something because it will stress you out or cause anxiety then don't do it. Don't bother about inconveniencing others unless it's truly important. Focus on spending time doing better things that are more fulfilling for you. Wasting time means that you will be letting go of other much more worthwhile opportunities that you could be investing in. Time well spent is very important. Be productive; take care of yourself and your loved ones. Find the right balance and take time to relax as well. Don't waste time on unnecessary things that leave you tired and unhappy.

Practice Self-Care

Learning to love and care for yourself is an important part of the minimalistic lifestyle. Taking care of yourself does not mean living selfishly. A person who takes care of themselves is more able to take care of others as well. A good example is when you get on a plane and the stewardess tells you in the event of an emergency to fit your own oxygen mask before helping others? They say this because if your struggling physically then your going to be no use in helping anybody else. If you don't practice self-love, you will lack inner happiness and as a result you will be looking for it from others. Why depend on others for something that you can provide for yourself. Self-care can involve the tiniest of things like reading a book you like, taking a warm bath or going on a trip once in a while. You may be working very hard to achieve your goals, but every now and then you need to stop, take a break and smell the roses or life will pass you by without even realising it. Feeling good and content will help you do better for others as well.

Appreciate Your Present

People have a tendency to focus on the past and future much more than they do on the present. You have to appreciate where you are and what you have currently at this very stage in your life. Ingratitude is an unhealthy attitude and only leads to negativity. Don't let your past or future engulf you in a way that you don't appreciate your present. It is important to learn how you can make the best of things at any point in life. This will help you survive and strive for better. Don't take things for granted; you don't know what the next day has in store or you. If you have a positive attitude and live in the present, you will be able to live a fuller and happier life.

Stay Strong During the Bad Times

You may feel like your problems are bigger than anyone else's, but there is always another person who has it worse. Don't be dismayed when you go through tough times; you can definitely make it through. Being mentally strong and resilient will help you get through any bad times in your life. There might be problems that arise from your personal choices while other problems may be the result of something completely out of your control. You still need to act graciously through it all and wait for a better day. Remember the sun will come up tomorrow and you will have another chance to better yourself. No matter what trials you face, there is always something that you can show gratitude for, the nice warm bed you sleep in every night or the simple fact that you can physically get up and go for a walk whenever you want. The bad times will help you grow as a person and also learn about what is truly important in your life. Remember you learn a lot more from your mistakes and failures than your successes.

Stop Chasing Happiness

You have to understand that happiness cannot be chased. You will not become happy if you buy that expensive car or your paycheck increases. Happiness is a mindset. If you want to be happy in life, you need to believe that you are happy. Lack of appreciation for what you have and wishing you had what someone else has will never allow you to be happy. If you make a choice to be happy, no problems in your life will take that state of mind away from you. You can always find the smallest reasons to stay happy. Don't let your happiness depend on others or any material possessions.

All of the above are some of the basic principles of living a minimalistic lifestyle. Try implementing them and changing your present mindset. It won't be easy, and you will find yourself falling back to your default setting of a "victims mentality" but the more you work on it the less that will happen. Minimalism itself is a mindset, and you have to transition to this positive state of mind in order to do better in life.

Chapter Four
The Minimalist Budget

In this section, we will deal only with money and your budget. You may be wondering what minimalism has to do with your finances. Well, trust me when I say that minimalism is one of the best things that can happen to your finances.

Money matters and always will but it should not be your source of happiness or grief. You just have to learn how to manage it in the best way possible in order to meet all your needs.

The principle of minimalism is to teach you how to prioritize what is important and value those things while getting rid of the rest. This principle of minimalism is not just related to what is in your closet or how you declutter your home. It also applies to monetary matters.

Minimalism encourages you to leave a job that is not fulfilling even if it pays you a lot. This may make you wonder how you will pay your bills then. You will have questions about expenses and how to earn a living again. Well, the thing is, if you want to lead a meaningful life, you should not be so focused on the amount of money that you make. Don't worry, I will tell you how to manage your money, but first, you need to understand some things. There are many people all over the world who earn a lot of money but are still not happy. You should not assume that you will be secure and happy if you earn a lot either. Even if you make a little less money compared to before, you will be happier at a job that you genuinely like.

It is not that a minimalist does not need money or has lost the concept of money. They need it and appreciate it too, but it is not the focus of their lives. A minimalist mindset will help you to change your priorities to better ones.

When I manage my own expenses, I try to keep things as simple as possible. One of the important things that I keep in mind is that I should never spend more than I earn. Spending more than you have is the easiest ways to get into debt. Don't buy things beyond your means just to fit the image set by others. If you earn a lot and can afford that designer bag, go ahead if you really want it. Don't buy it on credit just to show off. The average person has at least 3 to 4 credit cards in their wallets these days. The key word here is credit. This is money that you don't have and are taking as an instant loan from the bank. You will have to pay it back and with interest. Living on credit is a very bad habit and needs to be checked. Keep one credit card around for emergencies but cancel the rest. Remove temptation in the first place. It is common sense not to spend more than you have, but not many people seem to think about that anymore. Try not to be one of those people.

Creating a budget based on minimalism will help you declutter all your finances. You will be able to use this budget to prioritize on your personal financial goals. I'm not saying that you won't have to spend much money when your on this budget. It just means that you will be able to cut out any unnecessary expenses and put your money where it is really needed.

A minimalist lifestyle by itself will help you spend much less than you usually do. When you stop focusing on acquiring meaningless possessions, more money stays in your account. I'm not saying that you have to live frugally as a minimalist. It is actually a completely different concept. Minimalism will just clarify things for you and make it easier to manage your finances. This mindset will make you more mindful about everything you do, and this will include where you spend your money. You will learn to question the necessity of things before buying them on a whim. When you stop following the materialistic culture, your expenses will automatically reduce as well. You will still be spending money but on things that you really want and need rather than random things that you only want at that specific moment but don't actually need at all. This is how it is different from frugal living which demands that you spend as little as possible and live on the bare necessities. A minimalist can spend a lot on an expensive bag that they think is worth it but will stop wasting money on low-quality items that won't last very long or will sit there as dust collectors in their home.

A minimalist budget is not about using coupons and trying to earn reward points. It is about simplification of your finances so that they are easier to manage.

First, you need to change your mindset about money. Stop living on credit and beyond your means. Don't try to own things that you cannot afford. If you can't afford the full price of something right now, don't buy it. Keep it as a goal that you can aim for later. Don't pay for it in installments and create a cycle of debt for yourself. This is why I recommend getting rid of credit cards first. Don't act entitled to a lifestyle that you cannot afford. A little tip that I use is when I see something at a shop that I want I never buy it then and there. I always give myself a week, if I still want it in a weeks time then I might go buy it then but more times than not I forget about whatever it was as the novelty has worn off. This is an example of how you can want something purely in that moment that you don't really need.

You have to define what is valuable and necessary for you. You need to know what is unnecessary in your life and cut it out. It is also important to establish certain financial values. This means you should focus on living a life free of debt. You should have a goal for what age you want to retire. You should also create a budget for your income to know where all of it goes. Your financial values will help you in establishing financial goals. They will help you in understanding and planning how you can reach a certain financial goal from your current state. This will include a set amount of time within which you intend to pay off all debts. It will also include a plan for when and how much you intend to start saving from your income. Your financial priorities will also help you in determining when you can start using some of your money to establish a source of side income. You will be able to create a financial plan for the long term until you reach retirement. The 50/30/20 budget is one of the methods that will help you in this process. It is explained further in this chapter.

Start making lists of all your expenses and keep track of them. This will give you an idea about your spending habits. Spending money can be a careless act that is hard to control. I remember when I first did this I was horrified to see how much I was spending on takeaways for lunch over the course of a month without even knowing or realising it. When you do start mindfully tracking your spending habits, it will be easier to make changes. Try to make a list as detailed as possible so that every dollar is accounted for. You can then start evaluating this list. Ask yourself if you really should have spent money on each of those items. Did they serve or add to your financial goals? Did they make you happy? Be honest with yourself during this evaluation. You should remember and try to avoid any of the unnecessary expenses that you know you should have avoided. Sticking to a budget will help in this as well so that you don't spend money on the wrong things when you can't afford to. It will be hard at first like any other habit you try to break but trust me, when you see your bank account grow from pay day to pay day you will soon get good at it.

Make things simple for your self. Keep a single savings account and one checking account. The savings account is solely for saving money, paying off debts or your retirement fund. The other account is for all the expenses. Also, keep one credit card only. Keeping track, and paying off only one credit card will make things easier for you. Using multiple credit cards means paying multiple bills at the end of every month. Don't spread your money in multiple accounts as it just makes it harder for you to keep track of them. Keeping your finances simple will help in giving you more clarity and better organization. Another tip with your credit card usage is make sure your able to pay it off or very close to it every month. Making the minimum payment only is a fast track road to financial stress and once you go down that road it's very hard to get off that track.

Make a list of specific expenses with your income in mind. You have to break down all your expenses and your income and decide where your money should really be going. This list is not the same as creating a budget. It is a clear view of everything that you spend money on. It should include factors like mortgage or rent, groceries, transportation, entertainment, utilities, travel, children's expenses, etc. Creating spreadsheets will help you plan and keep track of everything that you spend money on in a month.

Automating payments for the necessary bills will make things simple for you. Minimalism is about simplifying your life, and automated payments are a hack you should apply. This way you can automatically push money out to any debt payments, bills, etc. at the beginning of every month.

50/30/20 Rule

One of the best rules to apply to your budget is the 50/30/20 rule. Regardless of a minimalist lifestyle or not, it is very helpful in managing money. As a minimalist, it will help you survive on a lower budget as well if you just use your money right. 50% of what you earn should be dedicated to the essentials. A lot of things will fall into this category, so its ok to assign half of your income here. These include all the necessary bills like electricity, rent or water that you have to pay every month. It will consist of your food and transportation costs as well. This percentage will generally work for everyone no matter how much or how little they earn.

After keeping half your earnings for the essentials, set aside 20% for savings. You need to understand how important savings are. They will help you through any bad patches financially. This category also includes paying off any bad debt or investing in any saving schemes. This amount may seem small at first, but considering most people don't have any savings at all this small percentage will slowest become a large amount of money. The earlier you start, the more money you will have set aside for retirement. You will also be able to pay off any debt quickly by setting this much aside from your regular income.

The last part of your income is for personal expenses. While the first half was essential, this is for unnecessary expenses. In modern society, these unnecessary personal expenses have taken a very prominent place. As a minimalist, you should start thinking about what you really want and should spend money on. This part of your budget is for extra expenses like drinking coffee at a cafe, Netflix subscriptions or your data plans. Adjust all these expenses within 30% and try to save as much as possible. This is also the category that will pay for any restaurant meals or trips so keep this in mind. Don't cross this threshold for personal expenses. The less you spend in this category, the more progress you are making.

All of these things will help you live on a better budget as you switch to a minimalist lifestyle. You will be able to save more money and spend in a more mindful way. Finances are one of the biggest causes of stress in most people's lives, I know it's always been my biggest stress and this is method is what helped me overcome this so I know it works if it's implemented and followed.

Chapter Five
Tips on How to Create a Minimalist Closet

In this section, you will learn how to give your closet a minimalist makeover. It will help you to streamline or downsize the overflowing closet that you currently have. The lifestyle philosophy of minimalism has to apply to every aspect of your life, and this includes your closet and what you wear. As you read on, the next section will help you build a minimalist wardrobe for yourself. But first, you need to declutter and make space for better things in your closet. The tips given here will help you in selecting things that you want to keep and taking out things that you don't need at all. You will be able to segregate items for keeping, selling, donating or just throwing away. After this is done, you will learn how to organize and keep everything in a neat and simple way.

We all know how hard it is to keep a tidy closet, but with minimalism; it just gets so much easier. For instance, everyone seems to have that one chair in the room that is piled with clothes and bags. People rarely make an effort to put things back in their closet or in the wash as soon as they come home. This is how chores pile up and organizing your closet becomes another big deal for spring cleaning; however, a minimalist closet is easy to maintain, and you will learn to develop habits that help you keep it organized and clean every single day.

To create a minimalist closet, here are some things you need to do:

Be Selective

Train yourself in becoming more selective about what you keep in your closet. It should be a space that is reserved only for things that you truly need and love. You should not take up any space for clothes, shoes or bags that you don't love or don't make you feel comfortable or good in. If anything doesn't fit well, get rid of it. This applies for any torn, stained or scratchy items as well. Only keep things that always make you feel good whenever you wear them. Don't keep anything that doesn't suit your personal style either. You don't have to follow every changing trend of the season. A minimalist wardrobe is truly evergreen and will look good no matter what the latest fashion is because you will rock it confidently. Your closet is not a storage room but a space for what you love and what reflects you as a person.

Individual Style

Be individualistic in the way you approach style. The latest fads are not your concern, and you should not try to fit in with the masses. You can go ahead and buy the latest bag if you really love it but not just because everyone else is buying it. Just because people are dressing a certain way, you don't have to try and fit in. You don't have to try and fit any labels either. A lot of people try so hard to dress in one particular style just to fit a certain tag like bohemian, gothic, etc. Don't try to do this. Wear different styles of anything that you like and feel good in. You should remember that your personal style is a reflection of yourself and personality, so cultivate a wardrobe that suits you. Don't let others dictate how you should dress or if something is out of fashion. Select fabrics that you are comfortable in. Get clothes tailored to fit you and don't stress about fitting into a certain size. Choose colors that you love. Also, keep in mind that the items in your closet are appropriate for whatever work you do or any purpose that you need them for. If you are someone who has to walk around a lot, there is no sense in buying a ton of high heels, and having no comfortable shoes is there?

Focus on Quality and not Quantity

Most people and especially women these days seem to think that having endless options in your wardrobe is ideal; however, this is not the case and is a waste of your money, time and space. Even when you have tons of items in your closet, you will barely use any of them. I personally use to have a closet full of clothes as well as a couple suitcases full of even more clothes, handbags and shoes. What was stored in those suit cases hadn't seen the light of day in years but I refused to throw them out or give them away because I was convinced I may need them one day. It was a crazy way to live. Don't try and buy too many things every time there is a sale, or you find some cheap clothes. We aren't saying that you need to buy high-end items every time and have to spend all your money on branded clothes. But you need to pay attention and shop mindfully. A lot of cheap clothes on sale are either ill-fitting or of cheap material that won't last long. Avoid wasting money on these things. Instead, invest in something that you truly like and feel comfortable in, even if you have to pay full price for it; it will last longer and work out cheaper in the long run. I went through a stage where I was buying a lot of my clothes on eBay to save money. This might have saved me a little cash in the short term but when a t-shirt looked like a pyjama top after 2 washes it would result in me having to throw it out and having to spend more money to replace it. Im not saying you can't go check out the sales when they come around but rather don't just buy it because it seems like a cheap deal. You have to invest in items of good quality so that they last a long time, look good on you and are really worth your money. Your clothes should be durable and not just something to last for a single season. A good minimalist closet has things that will last a very long time without ever going out of style.

Ignore the Latest Trends

You need to emphasize this point. Don't get tricked into buying things constantly just because others are wearing them. This is how the fashion industry thrives and they are the only ones benefitting from your constant splurging in them. You don't need to fit into a crowd or get intimidated by others. Wear what you please and have fun with your clothes. No one else should dictate how you should dress or which shoes are in or out of fashion. Having your personal and distinctive sense of fashion is what will separate you from the masses and make you a true style icon.

Experiment

Experiment more while cultivating your personal style and wardrobe. There are so many different styles that you may not have tried before. Use this opportunity to experiment and find what you truly love and what suits you. You can try all types of clothes, shoes or accessories to express yourself. Also, keep your lifestyle in mind when selecting clothes. As you experiment more, you will be able to find the type of styles that appeal to you the most, and this will help in building your wardrobe. Just because your closet should be minimal, does not mean it can't be unique.

Stick to your Budget

Set aside a specific budget for shopping. Don't carry a credit card or tons of cash and blow it all on a random shopping spree. Most people end up overspending when they see all the options out there. Before you go shopping, think of the things that you really need or want first. Then think of an estimated amount that you will need for those and only carry that much. If you don't carry extra, you won't be able to spend more than you initially intended to anyway. Don't go out of your budget even if you find something really great or if there is a sale going on. If you really like something then buy that instead of something else. Yes this means possibly leaving your credit card home and just bringing the cash needed. This will help you think before splurging unnecessarily on what you won't even use later. Don't buy in season clothes at a high price just because they are the latest trend. Most trends pass, and you will just be hoarding those items later. I can't tell you how many clothes I have purchased in the past that I either never wore at all or possibly just once before having them take up unwanted space in my closet. Think and invest only in items that you will make use of for a long time to come and are truly your style.

Segregate Clothes

Keep clothes for regular wear and others for special occasions. You need to think about the outfits that you wear on a regular basis. Invest in more of these types of clothes in high quality because you know you will really be making use of them. If you have any clothes that you haven't worn at all in 6 months or even in the appropriate last season for them, get them out of your closet. Don't buy an overpriced outfit for a single occasion that you can't wear again. Find something that you can definitely use for other occasions as well. Don't bother about someone seeing you in the same outfit twice. If you really love that outfit, you will feel good in it no matter how many times you wear it. A single piece of clothing can be worn in so many different ways and with various types of accessories. Experiment and make things fun for yourself. Prioritize and buy what you need on a regular basis first.

Tips to Declutter your Closet

By now you have a general idea of what a minimalist closet should be like. Before you start buying new things or organizing your closet, you need to declutter. The following tips will help you in doing this.

Take everything out of your closet first

Don't leave a single thing inside. Then give it a thorough cleaning. A clean closet will help in maintaining clothes for a longer time. When you are done cleaning, you can start by sorting through your items and organizing them back into the closet. Begin with making piles for your clothes. Make a pile for clothes you will keep, another pile for donation and another for re-selling. When it comes to clothes, you shouldn't really throw them away since there are many people who can still use them even if they have some wear and tear.

Think well about the clothes you decide to keep

Don't hoard something just because it was very expensive or you liked it at some point in time. If you haven't worn something in the last six months, you are not likely to wear them again. This gives you a simple way to differentiate between most clothes that you should and shouldn't keep. When you go through your mountain of clothes, you may even find something that you love and intend to wear but it was just hidden behind other items. Go ahead and keep these if you really like it but be selective, keep 1or 2pf these items not 20. When it comes to clothes for special occasions, check if they fit you and seriously consider if you still like them. If you don't, get them out as well.

Give away or sell

When you go through all of your clothes and finish deciding on what you will keep then begin segregating the remaining clothes in other piles. If something is in brand new condition or was very expensive and you don't want to donate it, go ahead and resell them. You will be able to get back some of the money that you initially wasted on them. You can also gift them to anyone from your friends or sibling who might want it. If you can afford not to resell the items, consider donating them. The needy people who receive clothes like these will truly appreciate wearing some good quality items for once. This will even make you feel better about yourself as it is a conscientious decision. Other than the resell pile, put everything away in the donation pile. There are numerous shelters or even your household help who might appreciate this; however, if something is completely damaged or stained, throw them in the right recycling bins.

Bags and Shoes

After your clothes, deal with the bags and shoes. There is no point in keeping any shoes that are hard to walk in or damaged. Check all your shoes to see if they even fit any more. Get rid of the ones that are don't fit and give them to someone who can wear them. If something can be repaired and you truly like it, keep it and make sure you take it in for repair. This way you will be making use of it. If any shoe hurts your feet to the point you can't walk from the car to your office without looking like your at the end of a big night out the get rid of it. There is no reason good enough to suffer for the sake of fashion. A lot of people suffer from back pain and even get injuries from wearing the wrong shoes. Invest in shoes that you truly love wearing and feel comfortable in. They should be the perfect fit and have comfortable soles. If anything is of a style or color that doesn't suit you, donate or gift these as well. If any pair is completely damaged, throw them away. This applies for bags as well. You don't need a ton of bags occupying space in your wardrobe. Think about the ones that you really make use of and suit a number of different outfits and keep those. Get rid of the rest as you please.

Accessories

Accessories are the next thing on the list. There are tons of knick-knacks that we collect over time. Sort through all the earrings, necklace, scarves and other accessories that you have collected over time. What really suits your style now? Keep the ones you love and can use with your new wardrobe. You can keep more accessories than clothes or shoes since they take up little space and are a great way to change how your outfit looks. Get rid of anything that is damaged or broken. Also give away anything that doesn't suit your taste but would be liked by your friends or family.

Organize

Once you have sorted through all the items in your closet to keep, you can start placing them back in an organized way. Allocate different places for each type of item. Use labels to help you sort through drawers better. While hanging up clothes, try to arrange them in a color-coded manner for better aesthetic appeal. Also keep the clothes that you wear regularly, more accessible. Clothes for the next season can be stored away and switched when the time comes. Keep room for any items that you need and intend to buy. If any clothes need ironing, do so and then hang them up. This cuts down on your dressing time in the morning. Clean all your shoes well before placing them back in the closet in an arranged manner. Use some nifty tricks to store and display your jewelry. For instance, hanging necklaces on small hooks will prevent them from getting entangled. Keeping accessories on display makes it easily accessible and you will make more use of them.

Once you are done, you should have a completely decluttered closet. You may be surprised by just how little you will be keeping when you are truly honest with yourself.

The next time you go shopping, don't buy things randomly. Minimalism will help you be more mindful in your spending. You need to avoid hoarding things again as time passes. A declutter needs to be done once in a while to prevent your closet from becoming a mess again. Don't toss in clothes without folding or getting them cleaned. Taking good care of your clothes will ensure that they last you a long time and you make good use of them.

Don't put your shoes inside right after you wear them. Clean out the soles to prevent any dirt getting into your closet. If you have running shoes that are sweaty and smell, clean them once in a while and keep them out in the sun to air out before storing in the closet. Don't let things eat up space in your closet. Your closet may up being large or small. I am not giving you any specific number for items that you are allowed to keep. This depends entirely on you, and you will learn to make the best choices by yourself; however, if your space is small, you need to be a little tougher on yourself and get rid of anything you don't need.

A neat and organized closet will be easy to maintain. Having things organized well on display will save you time when you dress up for work or an event. Another thing to keep in mind is that when there are too many options, it can be confusing and time-consuming. A minimalist closet reduces half the work for you and makes it so easy to select outfits on any given day.

With your accessories on display, you can play with your outfit according to the look you are aiming for. Invest in some refined accessories that you can wear for black tie events and use the other fun stuff to make any boring outfits better. You will soon see how accessories can really define your outfits. When you have sorted through all your clothes, you already know that what you wear on any day will be something that feels comfortable and looks great on you.

After every few weeks, you can repeat the decluttering to maintain this minimalist closet in the long term. Frequent decluttering takes lesser time and energy than waiting a whole year to clean out your closet.

The next time you go shopping, buy things that you really love. Invest in some neutral colored items that you can use more regularly. Find your own style and express yourself freely through your outfits.

You have to remember something, the number of clothes, shoes or bags that you own does not define you. They never have and never will. People who try to prove their worth by showing off their expensive possessions are not leading a healthy lifestyle and are lacking something. By choosing to switch to a minimalistic lifestyle, you are making a positive choice for yourself. Don't worry about repeating outfits or spending hours deciding what you should wear. People who compel you to worry about these things are not who you should hang around with. Establish a level of comfort and confidence in yourself to dress as you please and be who you are. You don't have to prove your worth by wearing the latest trends or carrying the most expensive bags. Stop worrying about meaningless things and focus on what really matters. These people don't pay your bills so why put so much value on their opinion.

Chapter Six
Minimalist Wardrobe

In this section, you will learn how to build a minimalist wardrobe for yourself. It will make it much easier for you to get dressed every day and even for occasions. People don't realize how much time they waste in the long run just choosing what to wear. The materialistic culture has also made it seem that you can't wear a single piece of clothing more than a few times. How many times do you see someone posting a picture on social media wearing the same dress? These days, the answer is never; however, you need to work past these things and build a good wardrobe that will work for you at all times. There is no compulsion to dress only in white or black as some minimalists do. These colors are just basics that make things easy. You can be someone who likes a lot of colors as well so include colorful clothes if they please you; however, don't go on a whim and shop all the time. Also, stop following trends that you are not comfortable with. Look at your wardrobe and think back to how many times you have worn each of the items in it. Get rid of the stuff that you haven't worn for more than 6 months as you are not likely to wear them again, this doesn't account for an evening dress that's only worn at functions that come up occasionally. Decluttering your closet will help you in this process. Once you are done decluttering, use the tips given by Wendy Mak to build a good wardrobe for yourself. Investing in this kind of minimalist wardrobe will cover all your needs, save time and save money in the long run.

Stylist Wendy Mak Rule of 30 Clothes

GOT a wardrobe full of clothes but always find you have nothing appropriate to wear? A stylist says you only need 30 key pieces of clothes.

"Most of us have way too much stuff that we never wear and for some people, getting dressed every day causes a lot of angst

"I found myself recommending the same pieces over and over again to clients so I decided to create a guide that can help people downsize their wardrobe to the crucial essentials that they actually wear day in day out."

The Capsule Wardrobe: 1000 Outfits From 30 Pieces. It's a list of 30 basic items every woman should own as a starting point for building a full wardrobe.

"I find that shoppers fit into two categories, "The first is a 'Sparkling Sally.' She's attracted to beautiful, fancy things and loves special pieces, but she doesn't have enough basics to round out that wardrobe. She has lots of random one-off pieces that are lovely but struggles day-to-day.

"But the opposite is 'Boring Betty.' She's got all the basics, but she doesn't have enough of the interest and to make it modern and contemporary and make it work."

We wear only 20 percent of our wardrobes and tend to buy the same pieces over and over, without thinking about what we actually need. Not convinced? Mak has a great trick to help you figure out what you actually wear.

"Every time you wear a piece of clothing put a clothes peg on the hanger,"

"After about a month you can take a step back and say 'These are the clothes that I wear all the time' and assess whether you need to buy more of those or move out the things that you don't actually wear.

"Buying the same pieces all the time isn't always bad. But if you find something that you love, like a top or a pair of shoes, buy them in different colours."

While you don't have to go full-on Marie Kondo and start culling everything, the 30-piece guide, listed below, is a great way to figure out what gaps are in your wardrobe.

"It's a formula, it's not prescriptive. You can adapt it and adjust it to your lifestyle,"

"You can swap items in and out. Say if you work from home or you're a stay-at-home mum and you don't need to go into the office every day, you could swap the tailored pants for jeans.

"Or if you don't wear high heels every day you could swap out a pair of heels for flats. If you work in a real corporate environment swap out some of the casual stuff for work clothing."

So here is the list of 30 items, along with shopping tips and suggested alternatives:

Bottoms

1. Jeans: Choose an alternate shape to skinny, if that suits you best
2. Casual pant in taupe or mushroom: Look for a casual pant without external pockets or embellishments, such as stitching detail, so you can dress it up if needed
3. Tailored pant in black: Select a style and cut that flatters you best
4. Tailored pant in stone or taupe: Stone or tape (essentially a few shades darker than your stone jacket) will work best, but you can also select cream, off-white, pale grey or a very light brown in a more casual fabric than your tailored black pants
5. Tailored shorts: Stone, taupe or mushroom shorts that are tailored and not too casual in style will enable you to take these from day to night
6. Casual skirt: Although a straight or pencil cut will be the most versatile, select an A-line or a drop waist if these flatter you better
7. Black skirt: Look for a skirt that has some detail so it can take you from office to play

Tops

1. Basic black tank: If you aren't a fan of black, select a dark charcoal instead
2. Basic white tank: If white doesn't suit you, an off-white or cream will do just the trick
3. A colourful blouse: Choose a bold colour that makes you look and feel good, and that works with both black and tan or cream items.
4. Another colourful blouse: Look to retail stores for colour inspiration and see what's on-trend this season in terms of colour
5. A coloured long sleeve top: Select a colour other than black or white to add interest to your wardrobe
6. A black long sleeve top: A dark charcoal will also work for those who don't like black

Dresses

1. A casual day dress: Keep any prints or patterns small and congruous, with a mix of light and dark colours in the print for maximum versatility
2. A little black dress: For both work and play, ensure the hem and neckline are modest enough for work and ideally look for a short or cap sleeve

Jackets

1. A trench coat: A classic coat or trench in a stone or beige will complement everything. If you live in a warmer climate, choose a lighter weight fabric and shorter length coat.
2. A black cardigan: Make sure this gives you plenty of shapes. It should not be too baggy and slouchy-looking on you
3. A black blazer: A blazer with a three quater sleeve will be easiest to match with jeans, as well as dressier items. It will keep you looking contemporary and young

4. A stone blazer: Once again, select a three quater sleeve. Ensure the shade of stone you select is lighter than your casual and tailored pants above
5. A casual jacket: There are many options here in terms of colour, so select in a relaxed style that will complement your accent-coloured blouses.
6. A black parka: Ensure that this is a proper, winter-weight parker for super cold days. Black works best or chooses navy or charcoal if you prefer.

Bags

1. A black, everyday tote bag: Patent leather will make this tote easy to dress up or down, as the shine adds depth and formality to the bag.
2. A tan everyday tote bag: For maximum versatility, don't go overboard with detailing and hardware on your bags
3. A small black clutch: If a clutch isn't your thing, a small shoulder bag is a great alternative.

Shoes

1. Black knee-high boots: A pair of patent leather will add pizzazz to any outfit. If you live in a warmer climate, select a small boot instead.
2. Black pumps: Once again, patent leather is your friend, taking you from daytime to night-time in a cinch. A rounded toe is more versatile and easier to match with opaque tights than a pointed toe.
3. Tan wedges: Co-ordinate the shade of tan to complement your tan tote bag. It doesn't have to be an exact match but it should be a shade in the same colour family
4. Black strappy heels: A T-bar is usually the most flattering style as it elongates your leg and foot

5. Dressy sandals: A flat pair of sandals in tan or bronze will complement your tan tote nicely, and it is much more flattering than rubber flip flops or sneakers
6. Black ballet flats: Whether you chose patent leather, a croc print or classic plain leather, you need a comfortable and reliable black ballet flat to run around in

Chapter Seven
Tips on How to Create a Minimalist Living Room

A minimalist living room creates a relaxing atmosphere for the entire family to enjoy and unwind. Do you notice how a clutter-free room instantly brings our stress levels down? Or the opposite - how easily we get worked up when we are surrounded by too many things... especially things that we don't really need at the moment?

A minimalist design is ideal when you want to open up space and make it look bigger. This type of design is appealing to most people. It makes use of simple functional pieces, clean lines, classic colors, and keeps you organized with various storage options.

Just because the design is minimal, that doesn't mean space has to look sparse and empty or devoid of personality. On the contrary, a minimalist design guides you towards a lifestyle that is essentially you and totally functional.

A living room is a common family space and also the one area that all guests enter your home. It does not leave a good impression on others if this space is cluttered and dirty all the time. Even for your own personal use, it is important to keep the living room clean and maintained just like any other room in the house.

To create a minimalist living room, here are some things you need to do:

- The first step in planning a minimalist living room is defining how you intend to use the room. Is it purely a sitting room to receive guests, or does it double to become the family den and entertainment room? When you know what activities take place in a room, then you can plan the furniture for the equipment that will be housed in that room.

- Choose your colors. One of the keys to a relaxing minimalist living room is clean and airy colors. Choose 2 to 3 colors, with 1 dominant color and 2 accent colors. Popular colors are whites, and natural browns and greens - colors that are found in nature. Bright colors are preferred over dark colors. If dark colors are used, they are often used as accents.

- Use a single neutral color for your walls and floors. Not only will this create an open space, it also creates a serene mood for your room. In terms of texture, plain and patterns in the same color can be used. Avoid prints.

- When choosing furniture, choose only the furniture that you need. Choose furniture with simple and clean construction. Avoid excesses like ornate carvings, fringe, and other embellishments.

- Curtains. You can opt to leave the windows bare. If you really need curtains, go for roman shades or blinds made of bamboo or other similar material.

- Lighting. In a minimalist living room, pin lights are the best way to maintain that clean look while providing sufficient lighting to your room.

- Smart storage. The key to a clutter-free living room is smart storage. Incorporate as much storage space into your design as possible. Clutter happens when there is not enough space to hold all our belongings. So planning for sufficient storage is important in a minimalist living room.

Tips to Declutter your Living Room:

A lot of people tend to keep their living rooms cluttered with things that they have acquired over the years. Every shelf is either overflowing with books or ornamental pieces or other small things. Over time you don't notice it, but now when you take a look around, most of it is unnecessary. Here you will get some tips to help you declutter the room before you get back to organizing it in a minimal way.

- Start by moving furniture and taking everything out from all the shelves and compartments. Keep everything in a corner and clean the room thoroughly. Make sure you move any heavy furniture as well since a lot of dust tends to accumulate under these. Giving the entire space a good cleaning routine will make it a much more positive experience for you. Make sure you clean the light fixtures, fans and air-conditioners as well. These tend to catch a lot of dust and need to be cleaned to function.

- If you have any thick carpets or rugs, use a vacuum to clean them well. Do this for the curtains as well. If your sofa covers are detachable, give them for a wash. You need to opt for some deep cleaning for your sofa once in a while.

- Now begin by sorting through everything from your living room. This includes the big stuff like furniture to the smallest little decorative pieces on display. Arrange furniture according to how you use them. If there are any pieces of furniture that you never use or are damaged, get rid of them. Be honest and don't keep them just because they cost you a lot of money at some point. You can even resell them at a yard sale. If your room is very small, get rid of furniture that takes up too much space. Switch them for more multi-purpose pieces. Make the most of whatever space you have.

- After the furniture, sort through the smaller things like books and such. If you have finished reading the books and don't intend to do so again, you can give them away. Donate them to a library at an orphanage or just gift them to a friend who loves reading. Giving away books to someone who appreciates them is not a loss. Keep the ones that are special for you and others that you make use of. You don't have to keep a pile of books just to prove how well-read you are. You don't have to throw everything away just because I am telling you to. If you are an avid reader who has a special attachment to books, keep them. Just be more mindful and selective about what to keep in your space. The point is to keep only what you love and get rid of the rest.

- Also, get rid of any old magazines and newspapers that have piled up. If you have finished watching all the DVD's and blue-rays and don't intend to watch them again, give them away as well.

- Get rid of any ornamental pieces that don't suit your style or are damaged. It is better to use a few great pieces that define a room instead of too many things that just make it look messy. Donate or throw anything that you don't need at all. If you want to use some of the things later, keep them in a storage area that is out of sight.

- Stop throwing your coat or bag on the sofa whenever you enter the house. You may be tired, but it is better just to go and keep them in the right place at that time. This way you won't have the extra chore of moving it later. There should be a coat rack to hang up the coats, and your bags should go into the closet when you are done using them.

- Don't leave remotes, keys and other small objects lying around. Use hooks and small containers to store them well. This way you are less likely to misplace them.

You can clean and organize your living room to give it a much fresher and classy look. Minimal decor is very aesthetically pleasing and easy to maintain daily.

There are lots of tips and tricks to making this room better. You can use vertical shelving to draw the eye upward in a small space. Use furniture with hidden storage to make optimal use of them. Place a large mirror opposite the window to make the room seem even bigger and to increase light inside. Various tricks like these will help you in applying a minimal aesthetic to your living room.

Anyone who visits you will admire how well you maintain your space. It will turn the vibrations in that space in a more positive manner and help in keeping your home a happy one.

Chapter Eight
How to Setup a Minimalist Kitchen – Things to Avoid

So as the first step in my guide to setting up a minimalist kitchen I thought I'd share the things I have in my kitchen that aren't minimalist and a list of things to avoid.

Before I get into list mode, remember that I know that kitchen equipment is a very personal thing. This is just my guideline and its based on the things that I like to cook. So please take this as a starting point and adjust it to suit your own preferences.

Things to avoid in a minimalist kitchen

1. Ice cream machine

It's no secret that I LOVE my ice cream machine. But since it's on its last legs and it's pretty un-minimalist to own one, I've been looking around for well-frozen desserts that have a similar creamy texture to ice cream but don't need special equipment.

2. microwave oven

I've gone with and without a microwave over the years and I've decided that while it can be helpful for defrosting things at the last moment and possibly melting chocolate, that's not enough to justify all the space it takes up. I haven't had a microwave for a couple of months and haven't missed it one bit. But if you're using yours every day, by all means, give it pride of place.

3. Stand mixer

A shiny, red kitchen aid mixer used to be high in my kitchen wish-list. Then I inherited my grandmothers gorgeous, retro sunbeam mixmaster which only runs at one speed – full blast. I haven't been able to part with it for sentimental reasons but I am finding myself using it less and less. If I want to whisk egg whites or whip some cream these days I use a simple old whisk and think of it as a chance to give the old arm muscles a workout. For creaming butter and sugar I use the food processor which seems to work fine but probably does lack a little in aeration. If you're a die-hard baker or pavlova maker a stand mixer might be worth the cost and space but for people like myself, it's not.

4. Knife sets

While they can look totally styling, and it can be handy to have a couple of good knives in the house if there's more than one of you cooking at a time – there aren't many people that actually need 7 knives of varying sizes. Save your money and invest in one excellent sharp cook's knife for each cook in the house and spend the rest on a good sharpening system – like the furi fingers. If you're a fan of rustic sourdough loaves like me, a bread knife is the only other one you'll need.

This is one area where I've always been a minimalist.

5. Bread machine

This trend should be well and truly past but I can't imagine there are many people out there who actually get much use out of their bread machine. If you have an oven and a pair of strong arms to knead you have everything you need to make excellent bread – and it won't be in a weird square tall loaf shape.

6. Rice cooker

OK OK. If you're cooking rice once a week or more – skip this point. But for the rest of us what's wrong with a good saucepan with a lid.

7. Pasta maker

I am guilty here. I go through phases making pasta but it's never more than once every few months. If I had my time again I'd be struggling to justify my shiny, Italian designed pasta machine. Fresh pasta is pretty readily available to buy now and it's not that expensive. If I feel like making ravioli I could always use Chinese wonton wrappers or cut down some fresh store-bought lasagne sheets to size. And I really wanted to channel my inner Italian nonna

– I could always use a rolling pin or make something designed to be formed by hand like these cute Frechette

8. Toasted sandwich press

When I was in college I had a little Breville toasted sandwich maker in my room and pretty much used it every day. I found that there was usually something in the uni dining room that could be half edible if put between a couple of slices of bread and given a whirl in the 'jaffel' maker. Roasted vegetables were a big favourite. I'd also use it to 'fry' an egg on the odd occasion. Since then I've hardly used one. If I want to make a toasted sandwich I use my frying pan and cook one side at a time, squashing down as I go. I find that toasted sandwiches may take a little longer this way but are just as delicious – even a little crispier because the steam is escaping as you cook – not being trapped.

9. Any other 'single purpose' small appliances

Juicers, deep fryers, hot dog warmers, popcorn makers, milkshake machines, chocolate 'fountains.' No explanation needed really.

10. Wok

I have a lovely heavy cast iron wok that my mum gave me years and years ago that I hardly use but keep it for sentimental reasons. I tend to do my stir-frying in my large frying pan because I find the heat transfer better than the wok – I don't have one of those flashy gas wok burner things. Of course, if you are cooking lots of Asian food a wok might be a better option than a frying pan.

11. griddle pan

Before I had a BBQ I got myself one of those cool cast iron pans with the ridges in the middle. I know some people swear by them but I always found myself with a kitchen full of smoke waving a tea towel in front of the fire detector. I'm pretty sure I didn't use the griddle pan ever again once I had the BBQ option. I sold it on eBay last year and haven't missed one bit

12. saucepan sets

I have a 3 saucepan set with a matching pasta cooker sized pot and a larger stockpot. Now, I like to make stock and often cook for a huge crowd so can justify the stock pot. I love my pasta pot and it is easily the most used saucepan in my kitchen. But the 3 saucepan set – I only really need one of them – Save yourself the guilt and buy your pots individually.

13. cake tins and tart shells in every shape and size

Along with little ramekin-like pots, and white plates and wine glasses this is probably my weakest link in the minimalist kitchen. Warning, this is going to take a while – 1 large metal muffin tray, 1 large silicon muffin tray (hardly used), 1 cupcake tray (was my Mums), 1 large rectangular tart tin with removable base, 1 26cm round tart tin with removable base, 1 20cm deep tart tin with removable base, 1 round cake cooler, 1 rectangular cake cooler, 8 individual pie tins, 8 medium individual tart tins with removable bases, 16 small individual tart tins with removable bases, 1 20cm springfrom cake tin, 1 x 24cm springform cake tin, a pair of sponge tins, a set of square cake tins in small, medium and large, 1 long skinny loaf tin, 1 fat (actually it's more big boned) loaf tin, I also have 3 flat baking trays, 2 round 'piza' trays and 2 metal high sided roasting trays along with a cast iron enamel le creuset roasting tray that is my latest love.

14. anything that is only to be used on 'special' occasions

I grew up with multiple dinner sets and crystal glasses that were only used on a handful of occasions. Life is too short people if it's good enough for Christmas day it should be good enough for a random rainy Tuesday.

15. mortar & pestle

Call me a mad scientist but I love owning a mortar & pestle as much as I love saying 'mortar' and 'pestle.' The truth is that it mostly holds the matches and doesn't get used often – it probably averages out to once every two months or so. I might keep it while I ditch my spice grinder (see 17.) when you feel like a homemade curry from scratch – there's nothing as good as a hand bashed curry paste.

16. anything purely ornamental

Useful kitchen equipment can be beautiful and decorative in its own right – I love my jar of stainless steel utensils sitting on the windowsill. But it's a working display.

17. a coffee grinder for grinding spices

Now I am known to rave about the beauty of freshly roasted and ground spices and it's true – they are more fragrant and flavoursome. But I can't remember the last time I roasted and ground my spices. Unless you're a hardcore curry head I think it's better to just buy quality pre-ground spices in small amounts so that you're buying fresh. Check out herbies.com.au.

18. expensive coffee machines

They always seem like a good idea at the time but most people I know go through their home barista phase and then realise that part of the joy of coffee is the ritual of going out and getting it made by a professional and their expensive machine sits gathering dust. Although if you live in the country it would make sense. Which reminds me when I shared a house with an ex-barista in the Barossa years ago. He had the real deal machine and grinder that took up a heap of space, but I did get quite addicted to my morning latte and didn't mind it hogging my bench space at all.

19. single-use utensils

Apple corer, egg frying rings, lemon juicer, nutcracker, strawberry dehuller (no- I didn't fall for that one) there are thousands upon thousands of little kitchen gadgets that may make life a little easier every now and then but in the scheme of things aren't worth the clutter.

20. electric carving knife

OK so It has come in handy, but since I've been keeping my cook's knife sharp, I've found that I usually couldn't be bothered digging through the drawer to find the blades and the base and put it all together and just use the cook's knife to carve.

21. mandoline

I'm not about to throw out my v-slicer because I do use it frequently. But is it essential? definitely not – a sharp knife and a bit of patience will usually do just as good a job.

22. kitchen blowtorch

I LOVE that I have the ability to make a real creme brulee but to be honest I wish it had more power. If I could I'd swap it for a real blokey, full-strength blow torch that I could then use brown meat and all sorts of things.

23. bamboo steamers

They were cheap. I've used them exactly twice since I picked them up about 3 years ago. Probably time for them to go.

24. multiple sizes of wine glasses

Sure, it can be nicer to drink white wine from a smaller glass, or even go crazy with different shapes for different grape varieties – fun for a restaurant but not essential at home. I'm on the path to having a set of champagne flutes (just because I'm a big sparkling fan and drinking it out of normal wine glasses just isn't the same) and a set of wine glasses that are on the bigger red wine side but I still have some stray white glasses but their days are numbered. I'm looking at a dozen of each because I sometimes have that many guests but you could just have enough for each wine drinking member of the household.

25. paella pans

They look so cute, but seriously, unless you are Spanish or desperately trying to become so, a large frying pan will do the trick.

26. tajine dishes

I do have a set of three terracotta tajines from Morocco. I did use them until the lid from the biggest one broke. Then I realised that the whole steam-swirling-in-the-conical-lid-and-condensing was a subtle difference I'm not sure I could detect. I now make my tajines in my Le Creuset dish and am happy to keep my tajines in the lounge room as a decoration.

Chapter Nine
How to Set Up a Minimalist Bathroom

The bathroom is usually the smallest room in any house; however, it is a space that we use regularly and for an important purpose: hygiene. If you don't keep the bathroom itself hygienic, it kind of defeats the purpose. Due to regular use, your bathroom can get messy and dirty very quickly. Most people also tend to hoard more products than they really need in this tiny space. Here you will learn how to apply minimalistic tips in a bathroom as well.

- The first thing to do is to get everything out of the bathroom. Take out all the products, towels, cleaning supplies, etc. from inside.

- Now give the entire bathroom a thorough cleaning. This particular space needs a little extra cleaning since you want to maintain good hygiene. Invest in some good quality cleaning products or better yet, make your own. It is easy to clean most things by making your own products using items like baking soda, Castille soap and lemon. Nonetheless, give everything from the sink to the bathtub a good scrub. You can also scrub out the dirt stuck between the tiles for good measure and to make the bathroom look brand new. Letting mold grow in corners will be detrimental to your health.

- Once you are done cleaning the bathroom, you can start organizing. First, check the space for the best organizing solutions. Use vertical shelves and make use of the walls. Attach a cabinet above and below the sink to store things away. Add a shelf above the door to make use of that space. Also, add corner shelves to utilize those small spaces.

- Sort through all the products and appliances from your bathroom. Get rid of any empty bottles or expired items, I guarantee you that you will have some. If something is damaged or doesn't work, get rid of them.

- Put things away in the right place. Keep the basics like shampoo, soap, and conditioner in a shower caddy by the bathtub for easy access. If you have extras, store them for later use. Don't pile things on the sink counter.

- Fold the towels and robes and keep them in the right place as well.

- If you have a lot of makeup, get rid of any empty or expired ones as they can damage your skin. Store the rest properly in the cabinet or in a makeup bag after you finish using them. Don't leave them lying around in a mess.

- Store extra toiletries like toilet paper above the door on a shelf for later use.

- Make use of small mason jars to store medicines or tiny items like pins. You can also add a magnetic strip on the cabinet door to keep the pins attached there. This way they will be easily accessible, and you won't misplace them.

- Keep all the cleaning products in the cabinet below the sink. If you can install a cabinet, add a shelf with a curtain to make it look neater.

- If you have enough space and a lot of things, organize them in small containers or baskets. Use labels to make things easier to find later. Don't leave anything lying around in the wrong place.

- Try to maintain a color theme in the bathroom. This will make the space look cleaner, and lighter colors will make it look bigger. It is also a good idea to install a large mirror above the sink for the bathroom.

Make sure that you clean the bathroom every single day. This can easily be done when you go in for a shower. You can opt for deep cleaning less often, but some basic hygiene has to be maintained regularly. Good hygiene will maintain good health for you and your family. Remember to put things back in their places and throw out any empty bottles when you are done using them. Being mindful every day will save you time later.

Chapter Ten
How to Set Up a Minimalist Bedroom

Your bedroom is one space in your house where you spend most of your time to relax and sleep in. It is very important that your room makes you feel calm. Even though some of us keep our bedroom really clean, we often forget the nooks and corners. And it's very common to keep unwanted clothes, stationaries, stacks of unnecessary books, old cosmetics, accessories and other things all piled up in our bedroom. We hardly even notice them most of the time. There are recent studies where scientists have proven that keeping your personal space organized and clutter-free does, in fact, keep your brain clutter free as well and it helps you stay calm and stress-free.

Whether it is because you want to be stress-free or get rid of excess things, which you no longer need. Decluttering your bedroom is going to help you reduce, simplify and find meaning in your life. It will aid in making you aware of what you have in your life and help you make conscious decisions to keep the things that are important to you. Here are some steps to help you organize and declutter your bedroom.

Make Your Bed

Set aside your time and always start with making your Bed.

It's great to start from the bed because we forget to discard items that sit on your bed most times like that old pillow you keep just in case you may need it for a guest. When your pillow has outlived its usefulness, you need to get rid of it and not save it for a guest. The same goes for blankets and old flat cushions. Get your recycle and throw bag ready and toss that old thing in it accordingly.

Revamp Your Wardrobe and Drawers

Decluttering and organizing your closet and wardrobe has been dealt with in detail in another section. Here you will just get a small summary with tips to make it easier for you when you are cleaning out your bedroom. This could be the most daunting task, whether it's a spacious, big closet or a small cupboard, more often we don't really pay attention to what we keep inside those locked cupboards. You assume everything you have inside that personal space are things that you need. While in reality, you may have clothes worn 7 or 10 years ago. It's time to say goodbye to the things that don't belong to your wardrobe.

- Start by putting all of your clothes out of the wardrobe in a free area or your clean bed. Leave them on hangers if you hang your clothes in your closet (this saves a lot of time)

- Once you've taken all your clothes from your wardrobe and kept it all in one place. You will see your clothes piled up and this is a good practice to help you analyze everything you own and how much you have consumed.

- Ask yourself questions like:

  "Is this necessary or is superfluous?"

  "Do I really think I will be using this in the future?"

  If your answer is NO then you can make use of one of the bags and toss it in the throw bag if its very old or has holes in it, the donate bag if it looks wearable also, it's always nice to wash these clothes before donating, you don't want to donate old dirty stained clothes.

- Select your clothes according to the season. Keep your winter wear and summer wear in different compartments of your wardrobe, or you could even store them in other places for instance: you could store them at the topmost shelve of your wardrobe or under your bed if you have storage space. Keep only necessary and clothes you think you wear daily in your closet. This will also help save a lot of time when you need to go out somewhere.

- Organize your underwear, socks, sleepwear, scarves, hats, etc. Keep what's needed and discard things that have not been worn for more than 6 months, feel free to toss old holed up clothes in bad condition into a throw bag. Check for your painless socks and the ones with holes and throw them.

- Keep dirty clothes aside, and it's always easy when you divide them into trousers, tees, dresses or shorts. The most important thing of all is to keep the darker clothes apart from, the lighter ones.

- Fold and keep your clothes organized. Shorts and summer shirts on one side and formals on the other. Gym clothes on the other shelf and so on. Scarves and hats on the other cupboard or another shelf. Jeans on one side and sweaters or jackets on the other. Keeping all your clothes mixed together will only make it stressful when you are getting ready to go out.

- Once you're done with cleaning out and organizing the cupboard, you will feel like you've accomplished most of the decluttering, but there's a lot more.

Organize Your Desk

- Whether you're a student, a person who has a 9 to 5 job or a boss, it is very important that you be inspired when you work. A clean, organized desk will make you feel more comfortable and fun to work.

- Start by organizing stationeries. Throw what's broken and doesn't serve any purpose to you. Organize your pens, pencils, sketch pens or sharpies and keep them all in different pen holders or a pencil bag. Donate things that work but is not needed anymore. You can recycle old notebooks and books that are not needed anymore.

- Clean out your desk drawers and keep only purposeful things in the drawer. Throw out unwanted chargers or cables which do not work.

Clear the Bedside Table

This area is where you keep things that are absolutely needed for you when you're in your bed, so it is very important to keep it clean and organized to get a good night sleep and also keep everything that you need in arms reach.

- Keep in mind to keep the things that you would need when you wake in the morning, and when you go to sleep in your bedside table, for instance, a bedside lamp has always been mandatory for most bedside table, but you could always replace them with decorative pieces or photo frames or scented candles which would look good in your bedside table without making it look too chaotic.

- If you're a bookworm, then it's always great to end the day reading a nice book it will also help you get a sound sleep. Keep the book that you're currently reading on your bedside table but no more. Do not make this a mini book shelf by stacking books upon books in this area.

- You may need an alarm clock on your bedside table for the next morning. It is always better to use an alarm clock rather than alarms on mobile phone's as this not only tempts you to check social media or play games which chews Up valuable sleep time, a much underrated part of our health. It is also unhealthy to wake up to a snooze sound.

- Keeping a bottle of water can always help if you wake up thirsty at some point in the night, you don't have to go to the kitchen for a glass of water at night. This also sets a healthy habit of drinking water the moment you rise in the morning where we are severely dehydrated.

- An ideal bedside table would be a neat bedside table with a lamp, a book, an alarm and a glass of water. If you have other things that you would like to keep, then it is good to store them away on a shelf or a larger unit.

- Adding a little bit of personal care to your bedside table is also a great thing. You can keep your lip balm or moisturizer if you're the kind who has chapped lips or dry skin.

Once your bedside table is neat and clean holding things that are only needed it's time to move on to the next.

Get Rid of Unwanted Accessories

Throw away old rusted accessories. Donate the ones that you no longer use. Unless you're a DIY artist, then you could recreate certain accessories into something else.

Throw Out Old Unused Beauty Products

It is very common for dressers to look cramped up with makeup products and cosmetics you don't use. Throw out old lotions and makeup if you don't use them anymore, throw out old dried out nail polish and empty bottles of oils and other beauty products.

Check your combs and other beauty accessories while you are cleaning your makeup table and throw out anything that is old, there's no point in keeping old electronic appliances like a hair dryer, straightener, curler, etc which don't work.

Get Rid of Unwanted Furniture

Any furniture that is not fitting well with your room can be relocated to another room in your house. It is important not to live in a space that's cramped with furniture. Keep only whats necessary for you in your room like a chair serves a purpose for you to sit and relax or work in. Shelves would be to keep decorative items you like or books you read. Throw out furniture that takes up a huge amount of space in your room. Once you throw out unwanted extra furniture from your room, you will see a huge difference in how your room looks and feels.

Get Rid of Unwanted Shoes

Shoes that are ill-fitting, old and worn out, or shoes that you no longer wear are not meant to mingle with the shoes you do wear and love. It is time for your old shoes to be thrown or donated. If you have useless purchases in your shoe rack, then it's time to sell them or donate them to someone who would love it.

All of these tips and tricks will help you declutter and organize your bedroom in a minimalist way. You will see how the room turns into a place where you can really relax and let go at the end of the day. Amongst all other rooms in your home, this is your haven, and you should strive to keep it so. Don't try to fill every shelf and corner with decorations. Keeping it simple and clean is the best way to go for this room. A minimalistic bedroom can really help you sleep better and also gives you a better space to communicate with your partner. Avoid bringing work or any stressful issues in this room with you.

Chapter Eleven
Tips on How to Set Up a Minimalist Office

A messy office could really influence your work performance. It is always very important to stay inspired and focused on projects while you're at your office but too often staying in a disorganized office can leave you feeling less inspired and anxious.

Start by decluttering your office desk. Decluttering your office desk is a constant battle- you cannot clean it one day and expect it to stay that way forever. It's important to make a commitment and take 10 to 15 minute everyday to declutter and tidy up your desk or set a day and time each week and completely dedicate that time to decluttering your desk. This will help you stay on top of the decluttering game, and you won't be lost with all the unwanted files and documents in your wild office.

Asking yourself questions can guide you during your decluttering session.

It can be really hard to get rid of items you've paid money for, so it always helps when you ask questions like if any of these items serve you a purpose?

Or if it's useful or functional? Or if the item is outdated.

Start by collecting all the papers lying around in your desk and drawers.

You will most likely find old cheques and bills, to do lists, and so many old unnecessary papers, throw them away or shred them if you own a shredder. This will be a satisfying experience. Keep the ones that are needed in a clear file. This will not only keep all the important papers together but also make your office look tidier and keep you organized.

Arrange the books

Collect books that are lying in your office in one place and see if you really need any of them. You can put all the books that are not needed in a bag or a box and donate them right away. The ones that you need can be placed in your office shelves or your desk in a tidy way.

Check Old and Unwanted Files

Check your cupboards and drawers, and you could find a lot of important files. It's important to keep them safe and in good condition. So, it is always helpful to keep them stored in a labeled box and keep them somewhere else.

Collect Miscellaneous

You will find all sorts of things lying around your desk and drawers. Ask yourself if you need any of them, keep what's needed and discard the ones that are not needed. Keep all miscellaneous items in a small box and store them in your drawer for the times when you think you would need them but remember to be truly honest with your assessment of each of them.

Collect sentimental items which are in your desk, maybe your family photo frame or a sweet note from someone special, keep them all in one place and once again ask yourself If they serve a purpose. It's hard to discard sentimental things, and it's harder to be ruthless here so take it easy. This is one area I still struggle with when it comes to throwing things out as I'm a very sentimental person. If your 50/50 on whether you should throw something out then I would probably hold onto it for a bit longer since you can't go out and re-purchase sentimental items if you truly regret it.

Decluttering Drawers

Divide what's in your drawers into pens, markers, sharpies, post its, etc.

Try out your pens to se if they are working, throw what's not working, keep or donate the ones that are fine. Keep only purposeful things in your drawer throw out things that are not needed in your day to day work life. Organize your drawers by keeping what's important, or the items that you use most often in the front of your drawer and everything you need less goes further away, getting organizers for pins, staples, pens, and other things can help you create an organized drawer.

Create hidden storage for your "maybe items." If you have way too many important files and documents or if you can't decide if a particular file is important or not you can put it all in a "maybe box" here you can store anything, and everything that you think could be useful. Label the box and store it on top of shelves or cupboards or if you don't have those, you can neatly place it under your desk. You can always find it safe there. It's a great way to keep the space looking tidy and also making a home for things in a more organized way.

Clean Out Shelves

Keeping office shelves organized with items that are needed and is of value for you can make your office look tidier as shelves display a lot of things, and a messed up untidy shelf would make the entire office look cluttered and very dirty. So it's important to store what's important in your shelves and also giving it a bit of personality would not harm, storing stacks of old documents and books in a shelf would make it a lifeless shelf. Adding your favorite décor pieces or a family photo frame can give it a bit of personality that could give your office space some personality. Storing items that are needed in clear-labeled boxes and placing them on the shelf can make the shelf more organized.

Just like the drawer keep things that are most important to you on the first floor of the shelf and the rest of the items according to how often you use them or if it's really needed. In this case, you can stack a storage box of old unwanted "maybe files" at the topmost level of the shelf.

Keep the things you need closer to your hands reach, and it won't harm if you'd like to keep one shelf for your pet plants. Shelves help add a lot of personality to your office room. This could also make your colleagues or visitor understand what type of person you are.

Don't forget the cables hanging around your desk or across your office. Computer and fax cables crisscrossing an office space is a disastrous site. First, check what office appliances are actually needed in your office space. Donate or give it to people who need it, if you find items that are just taking up space and are of no use to you. Carefully handle every wire of every device in a careful manner. Tape it below your desk or hide it with items you get at a stationery store. It will make a huge difference when you stop seeing all those wires dangling all around your desk. You will notice how it instantly lights up the space.

Clean Out Your Personal Desktop

We talk about decluttering everything that sits in a room but forget gadgets that are part of our personal space in this era. Decluttering your computer will make you feel lighter. Clearing out unwanted emails, documents and other unwanted files can make so much free space in your computer and also remove what's not needed for you.

Decluttering your entire space by throwing unwanted furniture's and electronic appliances could be a great way to cleanse your office to free up space and make it a more spacious workplace. A cluttered workplace with furniture lying everywhere or a working space with dysfunctional devices is not very practical. It is important to keep what's needed in an office. A desk and a chair would make a perfect office but if you wish to add more than two or three more items to this then that would be more than enough for office space. Keeping too many pieces of furniture or other excess items in your office can make it look chaotic, and an office should not give you a vibe like that. An office space is supposed to make you feel inspired and motivated throughout the day. It shouldn't be a place where you're lost looking for important items you cannot find.

Do Not Forget to Declutter Your Walls

If you're someone who hangs an awful lot of things all around your office room, then it's good if you take a step back and see what you like about each item you've hung in your office work. See if it's needed and if you really love it when it's there in front of you, changing the look of the wall could change the look of the entire office and give it an entirely new look and feel. If your someone that feels boosted when you read inspirational quotes and messages then you could hang one of your favorite motivation quotes on your wall, and this could help you stay motivated. The wall could even be a space for a great big notice board or a whiteboard for you to write your daily goals and future goals.

Make room for some personal belongings, you could make storage space for your bag, wallet or jackets, you could hang hooks in the room for your personal belongings. A storage box or basket for newspapers and magazines can boost your energy when you need to take a break and want to have a quick read on an article or when you just want to keep yourself entertained. Just remember it's 1 or 2 magazines and not a pile that will quickly contradict the point of all of this and that's to declutter your lie. Keeping a little storage box for snacks can also come in handy when you're exhausted with all the work and want to have a bite.

Declutter all the old Cds, USB and cables. Keep what's important and needed in the office and the rest of them can either be relocated or tossed away.

The next thing to look at is to make sure you label everything. Labeling things makes it easy to find things. Label everything. Labeling can be fun and also a very tiring process, but it is all worth it in the end. Label and stick everywhere. It will help you locate items you were looking for in a really short time.

After you have decluttered your workspace, it is now your duty to maintain it the way it is. Make sure to declutter your office every once in a while and everyday practice to keep what's needed and throw what's not needed.

Decluttering can be a lot of fun and can make you aware of the things you are buying as well. It keeps you mindful of the things you need and things that do not serve any purpose.

Decluttering your office space will make you feel motivated to work harder and keep you motivated long term. Organizing your office can make you less distracted in searching for important things around the place.

Decluttering is a wonderful practice and can be a relaxing exercise.

Chapter Twelve
Declutter for Minimalist

17 Simple Tips To Declutter Your Home

It seems like everybody nowadays wants to declutter. The very idea of only having the absolute essentials sounds appealing to most. And for a very good reason.

Decluttering is a key strategy for living a more simple life. Having and wanting less gives you mental clarity as well as the confidence to say no to mindless consumerism.

But whilst decluttering sounds easy in theory, many of us still struggle to implement it into our lives. It's often pushed aside to the "I'll do it later" list.

There are a couple reasons for this.

- You don't believe in the value of decluttering
- You don't know where to start

I'm going to assume that you already understand the value of decluttering but need some guidance to help you get started. By the end of this chapter, you'll have an actionable checklist of things you can do to declutter your home.

What you Need

It is very important to be conscious and aware of the fact that while decluttering your home and office that your things will end up somewhere when you throw them; hence you need four garbage bags, bins or cartons,(anything that could hold up items actually) one each for a different purpose.

The Throw Bag

Anything that serves no purpose or things you no longer need and is in an inadequate state can be tossed into this bag.

The Recycling Bag

Things you know can be recycled like plastic items, rubber, old clothes, paper, etc. can be tossed into this bag.

The Donate Bag

Always remember that someone else may always find joy in the items you no longer need so it's always great to donate to someone who needs it or any other organizations who would take your donations at any given time.

The Sell Bag

Remember that old skirt you never wore? It was either given to you by someone, or you purchased it while you were high on peer pressure.

We all make mistakes, and the best part about these items is it could be sold. What's better than decluttering and earning a little money while doing that? It's a win/win.

Declutter tip number 1 – Repack a Room

This is one of my all-time favorite decluttering tips from the guys over at The Minimalists. The idea is simple. Pick a room in your house and pack everything in that room into boxes. Over the next month, only take items out of the box when you need to use them.

At the end of the month, you'll have two piles. One pile for all of the things you actually used and a second pile of the things you didn't use.

Now you can make some decisions about the pile of things you didn't use and fast-track the decision-making process.

Declutter tip number 2 – Play with Numbers

Depending on what motivates you, counting your items might be an effective decluttering strategy.

I personally think it's powerful in some areas. A good example is clothes. It motivates me when I know that my goal is to have 3 high quality pants in my rotation.

Striving for 33 items of clothing sounds more appealing than simply saying you're going to declutter your wardrobe.

Having said that, if you apply this method to all of your things, you risk competing against others for the sake of competing, rather than focusing on the benefits of simplicity.

Declutter tip number 3 – Make Micro-lists

I love this tip because the lists can be very specific. For example, instead of creating one long list of everything you need to declutter around the house, you could make a micro-list of how you're going to declutter your kitchen cupboards.

When you break tasks into small chunks like this, you put yourself in a position for quick wins as it might only take you 30 minutes to declutter your kitchen cupboards.

Declutter tip number 4 – Set a Timer

When decluttering you can get lost in the details and sometimes it's better to make quick decisions to keep your momentum going.

Timing your task is a great way to get things moving along. You could set up a countdown timer on your laptop to help keep you accountable.

Declutter tip number 5 – Organise a Swap party

This tip is more for the ladies who have cupboards full of unused beauty products.

I know it's frustrating. You bought these products with high hopes, only to find that it's not for you. You hang onto these items thinking that you may change your mind. Guilt hangs over you as you convinced your husband or boyfriend that this face serum would change your life so of course it's worth the money.

The reality is you're never going to use these products again but you can't bring yourself to throwing them out. After all, you've barely touched them!

What do you do? Host a swap party with your girlfriends. Just because the products didn't work for you doesn't mean it won't work for someone else.

Invite all of your girlfriends over for a swap party. Everyone brings along their unused beauty products to showcase and sample. By the end of it, you'll hopefully have products that you'll actually use, or a the very least, your unused products wouldn't have gone to waste.

You can also do this with your clothes, shoes, and accessories.

Declutter tip number 6 – Discard Broken Items

This is a simple tip and one that should go without saying. I wrote this tip for the handymen and handywomen of the world who have the skills to fix broken items around the house but never get around to doing it.

Personally, I cannot relate as I'm useless in this area but I've observed the behavior of people who possess this amazing talent to fix things. It's a mentality of "oh I can't throw it out because I know I can fix it". Meanwhile, your broken belongings keep piling up.

Be real with yourself. Instead of putting these projects in the "I'll do it later basket", think about how life has been without this item. If it was really essential, you probably would've fixed it by now. So let yourself off the hook and discard the broken items in your life and move on. If you really struggle to throw it out, take it to the tip. Someone else may use the parts for something they are creating. It could just be the missing piece of their puzzle.

Declutter tip number 7 – Donate Books and Magazines to Hospital Emergency Rooms

Have you ever been to a hospital emergency room? Unfortunately, I've spent a bit of time in these rooms. The selection of reading material is usually 5+ years out of date. It would've been nice to see some more up to date reading material to keep my mind busy whilst waiting in an emergency room. Or at least some more variety!

Declutter tip number 8 – Roll your T-shirts

Decluttering doesn't always mean that you need to be discarding your belongings. Sometimes you just need to reorganize an area to create more physical and mental space. A great example of this is in your closet, specifically your t-shirts and tank tops.

Declutter tip number 9 – Cut Down Your Towel Rotation

I used to own 5 towels for whatever reason, but since becoming a minimalist, I've happily lived with just two towels in my rotation. That way, when I need to wash my towel, I have a spare to use when it's drying. I'm not sure why I would need more than two. Ladies might argue that they need an extra towel to dry their hair. In any case, if you have more than three towels (including one for the beach), you have an opportunity declutter.

Declutter tip number 10 – Organise Before You Buy

Before you race off and buy a bunch of storage boxes and hangers to help you declutter, take your time to organize first. You might realize through the organization process that you don't need any more storage facilities. I think sometimes we get excited about what our environment will look like once we've pared down.

Decluttering is not about design. It's about living intentionally. Only treat yourself to a trip to Kiki K once you've done the hard work.

Declutter tip number 11 – Be Realistic in Your Vision

Following on from the previous tip, try to be realistic about your vision. It's so easy to get caught up in comparing yourself to beautiful minimalist houses on social media and home decor magazines.

Yes, Minimalism is a sexy topic at the moment. And of course, it's ok to want to have an aesthetically pleasing house. You just need to be careful that you set realistic expectations for yourself. Your home may not look a certain way because of the way it's built, be it the materials for the flooring or the color of your walls.

Declutter tip number 12 – Designate a Spot for Incoming Paper

Papers often account for a lot of our clutter. This is because we put them in different spots — on the counter, on the table, on our desk, in a drawer, on top of our dresser, in our car. No wonder we can't find anything! Designate an in-box tray or spot in your home (or at your office, for that matter) and don't put down papers anywhere but that spot. Got mail? Put it in the inbox. Got school papers? Put it in the inbox. Receipts, warranties, manuals, notices, flyers? In the inbox! This one little change can really transform your paperwork.

Declutter tip number 13 – Scan Your Paperwork

Following on from tip 13, you could take things a step further and opt for a 100% paperless workflow. If you set up your system correctly, you can quickly scan important documents using your smartphone, store them on your computer or in the cloud, then recycle all physical paperwork. This is how we manage our paperwork.

Declutter tip number 14 – Sort by Categories, Not By Room

One of the biggest objections to decluttering is time and it's completely understandable. It's a daunting task to declutter your whole house. That's why it's best to break the project down into chunks. Typical decluttering advice will tell you to focus on one room at a time; this works for some people but may be too overwhelming for others. This means that delending on the room, you risk not completing the job within the allocated time. This sense of defeat can be enough to completely put you off from trying again.

Another way to approach decluttering is to focus on categories instead of rooms. So rather than focusing on the kitchen, have a goal of clearing the draws. Instead of focusing on clearing your bedroom, focus on clearing just your shoes.

Dealing with categories enables you to get quick wins. Furthermore, it groups like items together, making it easier to decide whether you can store, donate, keep or discard (refer to tip 12).

Declutter tip number 15 – Define Your why Statement

Making any significant change in your life comes from your own intrinsic motivation. Decluttering is no different. Decluttering at first can be mentally exhausting. It does, however, become easier, I say it can even become pleasurable when you know why you're doing it.

Here are some questions to help you define why you want to declutter:

- What is truly important in life?
- What kind of person do I want to become?
- How would I feel if I had fewer decisions to make?

Using these questions, write down a couple sentences about the benefits of decluttering and how it could impact your life. It also helps to establish some ground rules for yourself to help reduce decision fatigue.

The question I always ask myself when deciding on whether to buy or discard an item is, "Is this absolutely 100% essential to my life?" You will be surprised how often the answer is no.

Declutter tip number 16 – Chronicle Your Journey

The fear of failing in front of others is an extremely strong motivator. We see this a lot in the fitness industry, as people chronicle their weight loss journey and progress on social media.

You can apply the same method to decluttering. Embark on a 30-day decluttering challenge and post your progress pictures online for your friends and family to see. Your community could be the very thing you need to keep you going when you're not feeling motivated.

Chapter Thirteen
The Minimalist Approach, Clear that Clutter

The minimalist approach to interior design is all about clearing the clutter and reducing the elements of a room down to the bare essentials whilst at the same time retaining an aesthetically pleasing appearance in a room. Functionality, therefore, is extremely important as everything that exists must have a reason to be, a purpose to serve, a valid function. Minimalism works on the principle that less is more so it is all about reducing the elements in the room to a bare minimum, including any patterns, frills, and fuss, to create a streamlined, clear and uncluttered look.

The minimalist room will feel spacious and airy because it is filled with few items of furniture, which are usually spaced quite far apart and perhaps with only one or two ornamental pieces or paintings to add character and act as a focal point. There are little or no patterns to the fabrics, if fabrics feature at all, and no bright color contrasts or clashes to disturb the eye so the overall appearance is one of elegance and simplicity, peace and tranquillity.

If the minimalist look appeals to you, the following tips and ideas will help you create it within your own home.

Tips and Ideas to Create the Minimalist Look

Make a thorough assessment of the space you want to transform and what it is going to be used for. First of all get rid of everything that isn't required in order to make maximum use of the available space and fill it with as little as possible. Naturally, one thing to consider is where exactly you are going to put everything so good storage space is an absolute must. If you haven't got a lot of cupboard space already, it may be worthwhile installing some fitted cupboards and wardrobes.

Use paler neutral colors on the walls and keep them as clear as possible as this gives a relaxing and uncluttered backdrop to a room, a bit like a blank canvas, and will not clash with anything else. Furniture should be functional and comfortable with few ornate details and patterns. Floor coverings and surfaces, including tables, are best kept clean and free of clutter so texture and appearance of all surfaces are important considerations.

Conceal any wires and plug fittings that might be on view as these not only look unsightly, they will stand out and look out of place in an otherwise streamlined room. Limit ornaments to perhaps one or two key pieces to draw the eye and perhaps one painting or framed photograph carefully positioned on a wall. Windows should be unobstructed and clear so blinds or shutters instead of curtains will work well. If the window looks out onto an attractive view and is private, perhaps no window dressing at all imght be the way to go.

Light can be used to great effect in a minimalist room to enhance the simple, spacious and airy atmosphere or to highlight a specific area within the room like a painting, a table or some other eye-catching object. Avoid using too many floor and desk lamps to light the room as this takes up unnecessary space and adds to clutter. Dimmer switches are a good idea as they allow you to control the amount of light to suit the occasion and the mood.

In the bathroom make sure that all toiletries, toothbrushes and other items are concealed in a cabinet. Bedrooms should serve as a wardrobe overflow, clothes and other items must be stored in the wardrobe or out of sight. In the kitchen, all surfaces should be kept clear and if you haven't done so already, consider concealing kitchen appliances behind matching doors.

One disadvantage of the minimalist look is that it is very easy to spot when something is out of place because it relies on the fact that there is no mess or clutter so isn't really a realistic style for people who are not disciplined or who are particularly untidy or who like collecting and hoarding, it's more suited to someone who works on the philosophy of a place for everything and everything in its place.

Chapter Fourteen
Living in a Tiny Home

This chapter probably won't concern most of you as it's more for the people who want to take minimalism to the absolute extreme but I thought I would include a chapter on it anyway. This chapter is all about tiny homes. You may or may not have heard of a tiny home. Over recent years, they have gained a lot of popularity, and there are many small tiny home communities in different places. A lot of people around the world have begun embracing the concept of a tiny home. If you have the right minimalist mindset, it will not be a difficult step for you to take either.

A lot of people wonder why someone would want to move from a big apartment or mansion to a smaller space. The usual norm is to work hard and move to a bigger space as soon as possible. But will that really make you happy or satisfied? Does a big house define your success in life? I'm not saying that you have to give up your comfortable home and move to a tiny house to embrace minimalism. You can live right where you are or even buy a bigger home in the future if it is really important to you. For instance, if you have a big family, it would not be practical to move to a very small home. It is just another choice that you can or cannot make. Some people are suited for these small homes while some are not. If you are unhappy in a big house and don't need it, why not try a tiny home for yourself.

As you keep reading, you will understand exactly why people are opting for these small seemingly cramped spaces to live in. Living and trying it out for yourself is really the only way to understand if it is meant for you and how it will benefit your life. I will list all the benefits of living in a smaller space here. You will also get various tips on how you can live in a tiny home of your own.

You are not obligated to move to a tiny home just because you want to embrace minimalism. It is just another change that you can try if it seems feasible to you.

Tiny homes are actually not promoted much because they don't benefit realtors or builders as much as other homes. In fact, the features of tiny homes include solar power panels that are actually a loss for power companies. The only one that really benefits from moving into these small spaces is you. So if you want to save money and stop feeding the corporations, this is one of the best ways to do so. There are many more advantages that you will soon read about. You may not be able to comprehend this transition yet, but you will soon see why it can be a great one.

The Benefits of Living in a Tiny Home:

- Staying in a tiny home will help you save more money than you could ever imagine. Compared to the costs of buying and maintaining a big apartment or house, you will barely be spending anything at all. You can opt to buy a tiny house that is already constructed or get one made for yourself. Even then the costs will be a fraction of what the usual rates are. A tiny home is a much better choice especially for those who live in a rented apartment. The rates are exuberantly high these days, and for that amount, you can build your own home. It is always much better to own than living in a rented space. Instead of contributing to another person's wealth, contribute to your own. To be honest, the tiny homes may not be suitable for a big family, but for a single person, a couple or maybe a family with one child, it is ideal. There are some cases where even families of 4 live together in a small home. According to your needs, you can build a home made just for you. The initial costs are not much at all, and the cost of maintaining these homes is next to nothing when you compare your usual bills. A small space is also easy to maintain by yourself, so you don't need to waste money on hiring any help. In fact, a lot of couples actually build their tiny homes themselves.
- A tiny house is a much more environmentally friendly space than others. They require very little resources to maintain, and their footprint on the earth is also not unhealthy. For instance, most tiny homeowners opt for solar power panels as

it is sufficient for their needs. You don't have to pay high electricity bills to the corporations anymore. Tiny home communities also encourage the growth of their own food in order to be more self-sufficient and eat healthier. These people have embraced minimalism in every way possible and try their best to live a better quality of life. As they improve their own lives, they also aid the environment.

- You will be able to save so much more of your time when you live in a tiny home. Big houses require lots of time and effort to maintain. You have to keep cleaning and there always seems to be something to repair. There are unnecessary chores that are a waste of your precious time. A tiny home requires very little to no maintenance on a daily basis and helps you allocate time for more important purposes. You will have more time to invest in productivity as well as more time to rest and relax after a hard day of work. There is no need to stress about all the work that maintaining a huge house requires.

- Living in a tiny home will be liberating when you have to get rid of the tons of unnecessary junk that you have accumulated over the years. It gives you a chance to really see what you need and what you don't. You can always store a lot of stuff in a warehouse when you move, but the best option is just to get rid of them in any way possible. Material possessions have an unhealthy hold on our minds and lives. Reducing clutter makes life much simpler. There is no stress about moving all the heavy furniture when you move into a tiny home because it just isn't an option. Only take your bare necessities and build the house as functionally as possible.

- Building and living in a tiny home will be an experience unlike any other. Buying an already constructed home is an option but building one to suit your personal needs is the best way to go about it. You don't have to worry about the costs as you would if it were a regular home. Tiny homes don't require more than 2-4 people to actually build it. Most tiny homeowners around the world built their own houses. For issues like plumbing or anything you don't have experience in, there is always help available; however, most of the work can be done by you, so you don't have to worry about paying a contractor or construction workers. The materials required are also minimal so you can invest in high quality instead of cheap, poor quality materials. Use the house to express yourself creatively and to build a space that is uniquely designed for you.

- The cost of decorating a tiny home is minimal. As you embrace a minimalistic lifestyle, you will already be getting rid of any unnecessary excess. Use the space to keep things that you love and decorate as creatively as you can. Don't make it look cluttered and messy with too many objects. This will defeat the entire purpose of moving into a tiny house. When you don't have tons of corners to fill, you save a lot of money. Use this money to decorate with things you really love.

- There are no mortgage or loan issues with tiny homes. The costs of building and maintaining them are so minimal that nearly anyone can afford it. You don't have to take out a huge loan that you will be stuck paying for years. This will reduce your stress and help in financial growth. The idea of owning a huge house may be fun but actually paying for it can be nothing but a burden. A tiny house lets you get rid of these issues and really enjoy the space you live in.

- Your expenses reduce drastically in a small house and this, in turn, reduces the need to work yourself to the ground. Most people are so burdened with bills and loans that they have no option but to work as many hours as they possibly can just to stay afloat. A tiny home will not require that much money to maintain and you can work at decent hours that won't harm your health.

- Smaller spaces improve the relationships between people. When you live with someone in a huge house, it creates barriers and distance between you. It can seem as though you don't even live together; however, in a tiny home, everyone lives in close proximity to each other. It also helps you to learn how to adjust and be more helpful to everyone in the same house. This type of living can strengthen relationships and create healthier family bonds.

- The house itself will take very little time to build. You don't have to wait a year or so before you move into your new home. It can easily be finished in a couple of months, and you can live in your own home just as soon.

All of these benefits probably seem tempting to you by now as they should. People have the mistaken notion that a bigger home will mean more happiness and is a greater sign of success. A tiny home can actually be much better than any big house if your mindset is right and minimalistic. Minimalism teaches you to stop placing importance on material possessions. This only takes away from your happiness and does not contribute to it. A big house can be a bigger burden than most people can manage. Do things that reduce your troubles and stress. One way to do this is by living in a tiny home. All of the above-mentioned benefits can be reaped by this transition to a small space that may seem impractical at first but is actually great. You will save more money, reduce stress, save time and contribute to the environment as well. This is why you should give tiny homes a serious consideration when you embrace a minimalist lifestyle.

Tips for Building and Maintaining a Tiny Home

It is important to learn about the various details about building a tiny home. Learn from others experiences and use them to build the best structure for your needs. A tiny home will barely take a few months to construct and set up. You can buy one that is already made, hire some guys or even build it yourself. It may seem intimidating when you think about it, but it is actually not that hard at all. The following tips will help you in the process.

- The first thing to consider is how much space you really need. A lot of people cannot adjust to extremely tiny spaces and may need a bigger home. You need to consider how much stuff you are willing to let go of and how much you intend to keep. This will give you a general idea about how much space you will need accordingly. Offsite storage is an option for most of the stuff you don't need regularly; however, for all that you do need, there has to be enough space in your tiny home to accommodate them.

- Make a budget. You need to estimate how much you can afford to spend and need for your tiny home. The costs are generally very minimal, but it will depend on the details of what you use. Creating a budget will help you plan the house out accordingly. It is important not to go too much beyond your intended budget if you cannot afford to.

- Start devising a floor plan for your tiny home. You can get a good idea by checking the spaces that you currently use a lot in your present home. This will let you know which rooms and spaces are not necessary for you. It will also give you an idea about what spaces you need to mark off in the floor plan.

- Your plan for the house should be made as cleverly as possible. In a limited space, you need to make the most of every little corner. Use hacks that will help you create multi-purpose areas. Find ways to eliminate any waste of space.

- Just because the house is tiny, you don't have to reduce the size of everything inside as well. A lot of people think that the furniture inside the house also has to be shrunk in order to make it fit; however, you need to make sure that the inside fittings are made of the correct size. You cannot live comfortable if your bed is not made to fit you. Make good use of the space by making the bed a folding one or with storage. Adapt to the size of the house but also to yourself.

- A tiny house lets you think out of the box. Use tricks used by others but also try what you think will work best for your house. The same rules don't apply for a tiny house as they do for your regular big homes. Find out about the different properties of different materials to see what is best suited to. For instance, there are different types of glass that you need to consider.

- Use vertical space as much as possible. The walls are the largest surface in your home and should be utilized well. Set up shelves and cabinets vertically instead of horizontally. If you have kids, opt for two folding beds, one on top of the other. Even for yourself, opt for placing the bed on a higher platform so that it doesn't occupy most of the floor space.

- Fold down furniture is a great option. For instance, keep a fold-down desk in an area near the kitchen or window. This can work like your work desk as well as a dining table. When you are done using them, just fold it up again.

- Try to place a big mirror opposite the main window so that it reflects light around and also gives the illusion of more space.

- Opt for light colors when you paint the walls or even any of the furniture. Darker colors will block the space in and make it seem smaller instead. More natural light and light paints make space seem bigger and more comfortable.

- Make every space multi-purposed. Like the fold out desk, you can use other surfaces for different purposes. When you are done using the bed, you can fold it up and use that area for sitting or working. You can also use a pull-out bed that works like a couch in the day time. If you don't want a big sofa or such, use inflatable bags or bean bags that can be moved around according to your convenience.

- Try to install sliding doors to separate spaces. These don't take as much space as the usual kind. Keeping the sliding doors open will also extend the space and make it look bigger.

- Find out about different storage hacks that will help you make optimal use of your space. Use corner shelves in small corners, add ottoman seats that have hidden storage.

You should have a good idea about how you can build and design your own minimalist home by now. Living in a small space can be very liberating once you get used to it.

How to Keep a Tiny Home Decluttered:

In this section, you will learn some of the best tips and tricks to help you get use to life in a tiny home. All of these have been tried and tested by other tiny homeowners and will work to your benefit. Use them to build the best home you can for yourself.

One in, One Out Rule

A lot of tiny homeowners have tried this rule to help them keep control over their possessions in their house. Buying too much will just end up creating clutter in your home again. This can especially be a problem in a tiny home which has limited space in the first place. A lot of families in these types of homes have implemented this rule and found it useful. The principle is to get rid of anything that is already there if you want to bring in something new. This makes it necessary for the person to think about it before buying something. They have to consider if it is important enough to get rid of another item and replace it. Even if you don't live in a tiny home, you can try implementing this rule in your house.

Fixed Number of Possessions

You can fix a certain number of possessions that every person in your home is allowed to have. This number should apply to everyone including yourself and encompasses all personal belongings. For instance, no one should have more than 40 things that are just theirs in the house. If they want to get something else, they will have to get rid of something already there. The principle is similar to the one in and one out rule. The only difference is that there is a fixed number given here from the beginning. This rule can be quite limiting and hard for some to follow but will be quite beneficial in the long run. When you are only allowed to own a certain number of things, you become more conscious about what is important for you.

Assign Areas

Another trick to get accommodated to your new home is to assign each area for a different purpose. You can do this by creating small labels or just using sticky-notes. When you place them in a certain location or on drawers or cabinets, it makes you remember what that area is meant for. With limited space, you also have to be more mindful about what you assign a space for so that it is not wasteful. When you do this, you realize how much space you wasted in your big house and that you did not really need it.

Storage Bins

Another trick to assign space for everyone's personal stuff is using storage bins. If you give a large storage bin to each person, they should not own more personal possessions in the house than what fits in the bin. These bins act like a clear marker of exactly how much space is allowed for each person. If it doesn't fit in the bin, it needs to go out.

Use and Give Away

You can use certain things and give them away once you are done using them. For instance, if you buy a book, read it and then give it to someone else to read once you are done. This applies to any other object as well. If you know that you have no further use for something, don't let it occupy space in your home. Give it to someone else who can really make use of it. This is a good way to prevent hoarding and also encourages a giving nature.

As you build your tiny home or move into it, you will see how you took your large spaces for granted before. You will also see that it is not really necessary to have a big home and you should not limit your happiness to the possession of one. A tiny home can be very liberating as it takes much less time to maintain and does not cause any financial strain on you either. You will learn how to live more mindfully in your home and also be more considerate about the people you live with. It will also be much easier to keep it de-cluttered and this makes the space minimal and peaceful. The only way you can truly understand the benefits of a tiny home is by living in one.

Chapter Fourteen
Challenges in Minimalism And How to Overcome Them

Living a minimalist lifestyle is not as hard as it may seem, but it is not always easy either. You need to appreciate this and embrace it. It is important to understand that the effort to make this transition will be worth it in the end.

Taking the initiative to read about minimalism is a positive first step that you have already taken. Implementing everything may be a little challenging at first, but it takes time to break old habits. The materialistic lifestyle you lead today is the bad habit that you need to break. The process may not be easy, but it is something that has to be done if you want to lead a happy and fulfilling life. Making these changes will be hard initially, but they are aimed at making your life easier in the long run.

Breaking the current cycle is important in order to start a healthier and happier cycle of living.

A lot of people say they are minimalists or intend to be. Painting your walls white and wearing monochrome clothes does not make someone a minimalist. Just the intention of leading a minimalist lifestyle is not enough either. Your intentions need to be converted to actions. Your idea about minimalism needs to be clear and truly include its essence.

You might just delve into minimalism on an impulse like a lot of people do. The difference between them and you is that you are making an effort to understand it truly. I hope this book helps you out in this. But you need to really start implementing the steps suggested here and make it your lifestyle.

Decluttering and throwing some things away will not make you a minimalist. A lot of people declutter once and just get back into the old swing of things. If you do this, your home or any space will revert back to the state it already was. Decluttering has to be done on a regular basis, and you need to understand that the whole point is to get rid of excess every single day. The first time you clean your house, it can be tiring, but you are motivated enough to carry it through. Seeing a clean house at the end of it will be worth the effort. But will you be able to maintain it this way for the long run?

Most people hate cleaning up and leave it till they absolutely have to. The process of decluttering and setting up a minimalist space is to help you in this. If you learn to maintain it and make a minimum effort on a regular basis, there will barely be anything to do; however, if you just start piling clothes on the chairs or buying more stuff again, the whole purpose is lost.

The problem is not the items that I am asking you to get rid of. The issue lies with your habits and mindset. You are asked to throw out the excess to help you see that they are not important in your life. You don't have to spend so much time and effort in acquiring meaningless things like these; however, this is easier said than done and understood.

The current mindset of people is a result of many years. As children, we are given a reward for a job well done or just when we behave well. This could be a new toy or some candy. In school, the rewards come in the form of books or certificates. In your job, you get a higher paycheck, promotion or maybe even a car. This makes you associate happiness and success with such material things. If you have been brought up to think this way all your life, suddenly switching over will obviously be a challenge; however, it is a challenge you have to take.

No matter how many clothes, shoes, cars, etc. you buy, they will only provide temporary satisfaction. Material possessions are not the way to attain real happiness. Don't buy things mindlessly just to get that momentary satisfaction. Why not strive for more and learn how to be permanently and truly happy? Minimalism will help you with this.

Decluttering is part of the process of implementing minimalism, but it is only a fragment of it. You need to prepare yourself for the rest and not just leave it at a cleaner house. You need to start living with intention at every point and be mindful in all your actions. Are you ready to do this? It is easy to think about it but not so much when you actually have to do it.

Your body and your mind will initially resist change, which is the way of life. How can it accept such a drastic change overnight when you have lived completely differently all your life? The life you have been living all these years is very different from an essentially minimalist life. You will only realize this when you start making the required changes. The most important change has to be in your mindset. You will be able to get through this initial adaptation period if you stay determined and persevere through it all. It's like anything in life, it requires effort, but the more you practice the better you get. Don't expect it to be easy or instantaneous. You cannot just decide and become a minimalist the next day. It will require changes in everything you do and how you think all the time. At first, these changes have to be intentional, but with time they will become a habit and your new lifestyle.

The reality of this transition to a minimalist lifestyle is that all your actions have to be thought through and you have to fight all your natural compulsions. You won't be able to buy those shoes at the mall just because they look good. You need to think if they are really worth it, if you need them and if you would be willing to give something else up in order to make space for these in your closet. This constant mindfulness will make a huge difference in your life. Not to mention, you will be saving a lot more money as well. Impulsive and unnecessary shopping is one of the easiest and worst ways to burn a hole in your wallet. Before, you probably just bought things because you liked them or even as a form of retail therapy. As a minimalist, your sense of satisfaction should not come from these meaningless sources. I'm not saying that you aren't allowed to shop at all, you just have to reduce the need to do it. This change will allow you to question everything that you do and as a result do things better.

You have to understand that there are no specific prohibitions that are being placed on your life. You don't have to own only 50 items to be considered a minimalist. You are not forbidden to go shopping or to own an expensive house. You are just being encouraged to stop depending on these things to be happy. Placing some rules, in the beginning, will just work to your benefit. Any numbers or tips are just to give you an idea and guide you in the initial stages. As you develop a minimalist mindset, it will become second nature to you. You need to give it time and stay patient through the process. The change can be easier for some than others but don't back off just because it is a little extra work.

This transition will be made harder by a number of external factors. There are so many options in every store we walk into. This can be a clothing store or even a food store. Even if you go to buy some cleaning supplies, there are too many options to choose from. Every time you turn on the tv or look at a billboard, there will be an advertisement convincing you to buy something or the other. These may tell you that you just have to have them, but you should know that you don't. Needs and wants are different. You can have both, but they should not be decided by someone else. People actually need a bare minimum, and when you start living minimally, you will be able to realize this. I'm not telling you to give up everything you want and just keep what you need either. A minimal mindset will make you think about what it is that you really want. In your current state of mind, you probably don't even know what you want. Stop wanting or craving for what someone else owns. You don't need to buy the same smartphone or bag that your friend has. The ones you own are more than good enough and serve the same purpose. Don't let yourself get affected by meaningless things. Even children these days suffer from depression due to the impact of negative thinking. Kids are bullied in school if they don't dress like their peers or have an older model phone. If you want to set an example for your own children or anyone else, you need to lead by example.

It's not about how many clothes you are willing to give up or how small your new house is. This is not what defines minimalism or you. It is about how much importance you place by those things. You need to stop depending on these materialistic factors for your happiness. There is so much more that is important and can really make you happy in life.

When you start leading a minimalist lifestyle, you may go astray after a certain point. It is very easy to fall back on old habits; however, don't let this discourage you. As soon as you see any of these signs, you should make a conscious effort to get back on track. One step back does not mean you cannot take two steps forward again. Consumerism is ingrained in the present society, and it can be hard to overcome it. Just keep reminding yourself why you are doing this in the first place. It may be because you wanted more free time or just to save money. Regardless of the reasons, keep reminding yourself and push yourself forward. You already know that the materialistic culture has done nothing positive for your life or mental health. If you want to overcome these hurdles, you need to be consistent in your efforts.

You can always look for support and inspiration from others. You can follow the example set by others who embraced minimalism and are leading happier lives. Looking at them will make you feel re-motivated and encouraged again. Watching others lead perfect lives on social media is not the kind of encouragement you are looking for. Most of that is just for show and barely the tip of the surface. Meet more people and have actual conversations; this is how you can learn from them. Take tips from the people you admire and whom you see truly leading by example. Take your time and set your own pace. You will get there just like anyone else.

A minimalistic lifestyle goes against the usual norms, and you may face criticism from others. Don't let this affect you. People are not comfortable with change and even less willing to see the fault in their own way of living. This should not concern you as your life is yours to live. As long as you are not harming or affecting someone else, their opinions are of no consequence to your personal choices. You may even face some resistance in your own home, but this will be easier to deal with. You have to remember not to impose your thinking or way of living on others. You should sit and explain what you are doing to your friends or family. This will help them understand it better. If they are convinced, they may join you in the journey or even follow later. Don't impose it on them just because you want it. If you share a space with others, keep their needs in mind too. Don't throw things out without asking them first. You can do as you please in your personal space but not with someone else's things. Adjust to the needs and wants of others. The important thing is how you act and think about yourself. Over time as the benefits of this lifestyle become visible in your life, you will see even more people ask for your advice and follow in your footsteps.

Minimalism has been embraced by many people all over the world; however, the majority is still amongst those who haven't. You have to keep this in mind and be prepared for it; however, any change that you make in your mindset and lifestyle is for yourself. It is important to make these changes so that you can see improvement in your life. You can encourage others to try it, but the rest will be up to them.

Chapter Fifteen
Being a Minimalist on a Holiday

The holidays are usually a time of excess for everyone. People eat richer food and lots of it. There's a lot of alcohol and desserts involved. Shopping takes over maximum precedence during this time of the year as well. The materialistic culture that minimalism teaches you to avoid is at its peak during the holidays. This is why this section is meant to help you deal specifically with the holidays in a minimalist mindset.

When you make the transition to a minimalist lifestyle, it makes it easier for you to deal with the holidays in a much healthier and happier way. Most people get overwhelmed with all the money they have to spend on gifts, travel, decorations, etc. during the holidays. Then there is the guilt that comes once the season has passed. Can you really enjoy and be happy with all this? The true essence of the holidays has been lost over the years and minimalism will help you regain this. You will learn how to make things simple and meaningful again. The holidays are about traditions and family, not about consumerism.

Some simple steps will help you make the holiday season less stressful and more joyful.

- Let's start with decorations. You don't have to make it a competition with your neighbors and go all out on your house. Don't go and buy some expensive tree or decorations either. Instead, encourage everyone in the family to make their own decorations themselves. There are so many nice crafts that children will enjoy and it can be a fun activity for adults to take part in as well. These decorations will be much more meaningful and also save you a lot of money. Not to mention, it will be more unique than anyone else.

- Gifting is one of the major stressors during the holiday season. You can either stop the practice itself or make it a better one.

If you want to stop exchanging gifts, send out a message to the people who usually give you gifts. Let them know that you won't be buying anything and they should do the same. We stopped this a few years back and only buy for kids in the family and believe me it has saved us a large amount of stress and money. If you like the practice of giving gifts, do it in a better way. Over the years, the holidays have become a sort of gifting extravaganza. No one is happy with just one small gift, there has to be a pile under the tree with their name on it. Stop spending your hard earned money on meaningless gifts this year. You don't have to buy expensive things out of obligation. Put more thought into your gifts and buy something that the other person really loves or needs. This can be anything small or big but it should be thoughtful. Better yet, make something for them. Bake a batch of their favourite cookies or cupcakes, knit a scarf if you're good at it. There are so many ways to show you care without spending unnecessarily.

- Take time to relax and really enjoy yourselves during the holidays. Don't over-book yourself and say you will attend every single party you are invited to. By the end of the week, you will be left exhausted and unhappy. Go meet the people whose company you really enjoy and say no to the rest. You don't have to make any false excuses either. Put yourself first and do what is better for you. You shouldn't have to constantly worry about what someone else will say or think about you. You can stay home if you like or go out if you please, the decision should be yours to make. You don't have to make any commitments that you don't want to keep.

- Don't spend beyond your budget just because it is the holidays. You may need to adjust your budget a little bit to accommodate some extra expenses, but there should be a limit for that. Create a budget and stick to it. Over-spending will just make you regretful at the end of the season.

- Don't go on a shopping spree just because holiday sales are being held. You should be more mindful about what you spend by now. Just because the prices are cut down does not mean you have to go and buy as much as possible. You can definitely shop a little if you normally hold off on such expenses or had your eye on something for a long time. The best way to avoid excess shopping is to make a list from before and note down all the things you really want or need. Stick to this list and avoid anything else.

- Be more mindful about how you spend your time. Don't make too many commitments or constantly go from one thing to the other. It won't give you the chance to enjoy the holidays or spend it with the people who matter.

- Don't compare your holidays with against others. Your friends or colleagues may be going on an exotic vacation, but this does not mean that their holidays are better. Your priorities and mindset should be different. Be grateful for whatever you have and however, you get to spend your holidays. It is common for people to feel envy over what others are doing these days. You may see them post pictures or show off about where they are, what they bought, etc. This should not be a cause of your own discontentment. It is important to push away these negative feelings and stay happy with what you have.

- If you are not someone who likes traditions, you don't have to follow them. There is no point in doing something that you don't love. Spend your holidays in a way that makes you happy, not by the traditions that others enjoy.

- Avoid overeating and using the holidays as an excuse. Most people are left with holiday guilt after the season is over. They diet and exercise all year round and end up binging during this time. You don't have to eat excessively to enjoy the holidays. All the rich food will still be there but you need to eat healthy portions. Why eat more than your body needs or can tolerate? You will only end up gaining weight or falling sick. I know I struggled with this for a long time, If you eat in a healthier way, there won't be anything to be distressed about later.

- Start practicing better rituals for the holidays. Don't let everyone huddle around the tv to r play video games all day. Find activities that everyone can enjoy and take part in together. Take this time to communicate and share things with your loved ones. We don't do this anywhere near enough in this day and age with technology playing such a massive role in our lives.

You can come up with many great ideas to make the holidays better by yourself. Don't try too hard to create a perfect holiday defined by others. Your ideal holiday should be what you really want it to be like and what you will not regret at the end of them. Not what it should look like to others. A minimalist lifestyle will help you change your priorities and enjoy the holidays in a much more positive way. Materialism should not be the core of them.

Chapter Sixteen
How to Practice Minimalism with Your Smartphone

Minimalism is aimed at helping you improve your life in every way possible. If you are honest with yourself, you will accept that you spend an unhealthy amount of time with your smartphone. There's nothing to feel guilty about since this is true for every single person out there these days. However, this does not mean that you don't need to change.

Smartphones help in making your life much easier and convenient. You can do so much with one little device in your hand now. You can place a voice or video call to someone on the other side of the world. You can send messages and emails at any time. You have constant access to all social media platforms. There are various tools like calendars and reminders to help you schedule and keep track of your day. You can read books or watch movies on your phone. There is just so much that can be done and this has made it easy for us to be completely absorbed by these devices. There is a limit to which you should be using a smartphone, and your dependency on it should not cross that limit.

A smartphone is just another materialistic object that may be important but is not something you should be using the whole day. It is okay to reply to texts a little late or call someone back when you are free. You don't have to make yourself constantly accessible to everyone. The convenience provided by smartphones is a privilege that you should appreciate and not take for granted. It is not something you should be unhealthily obsessed with. Studies show that the average person feels a certain level of anxiety if they don't have access to their smart-phone for more than an hour or so. Do you think this level of dependency is healthy for you? As a minimalist, you need to make an effort and reduce your attachment to materialistic things such as this.

Let's talk about how much money you spent on your smartphone. There are new models being launched all the time, and everyone always wants the latest ones. The prices also keep rising, and you probably spent a large amount of your income on various phones over the years. However, most people change their phone even when their previous one is perfectly functional. Is there something in the new model that really sets it apart from the older one? If not, why are you willing to spend so much of your hard earned money on something that works the same but just looks a little different. This is the result of a materialistic culture that you need to detach yourself from.

All the functions and applications in a smartphone definitely make life easier. However, you need to take steps to reduce this dependency. If you try to keep your phone off for an entire day, you will notice just how uncomfortable and anxious it makes you. However, it is something you should try. It may be tough, but it is not impossible. Just try staying without your phone for a few hours every day, and it will get easier. This will give you time and better focus on other productive things.

Go through your phone and see all the applications you have. Think carefully about the ones you really need and which help you in becoming more productive. Get rid of the rest. Most of the useless apps in your device will actually affect the performance of your device and eat up space. Deleting these apps will save you time and improve the functioning of your device too.

Analyze the apps that you spend the most amount of time on every day. Most people spend too much time in their day using social media apps. Social media can be useful and makes it easy for us to stay connected with each other. However, over the years, it has had an extremely negative impact on the mental health of users. There has to be a limit to how much you use social media. If you can't exercise this control, be hard on yourself and delete them. Social media can be like an addiction that you really need to cut off from. Have you noticed how it has affected your thoughts about yourself, your lifestyle and your body? Seeing edited and seemingly perfect pictures of other's lives can have a very negative impact on your mind. You need to remember that people only display the best version of themselves to the world. They also have issues or problems like any other person. Don't let Instagram posts leave you with any illusions about perfection. Stop spending hours in your day lurking and checking what someone else is doing. Spend this time productively to do better for yourself. An example it the time it took me to write this book, I would never have had the time to write a book like this with the way I use to live. I spent every spare moment I had on Instagram, Facebook and YouTube. I achieved nothing from this. I know check my Facebook first thing in the morning and then before bed, I leave the rest of the day for things that actually keep me moving forward in life.

Delete all the various shopping apps on your phone. Just because you have easy access to stores does not mean you can go on a whim and spend money as you please. Adding things to your cart on phone applications can be an easy way to waste your money.

Keep your home screen simple and clean. Don't flood it with a ton of unnecessary apps. Add the calling app, calendar and any other utility app that you need constantly. Any other app should be on another page. Every time you turn on your phone, the home screen should remind you what the real purpose of the device is. It is not for you to waste hours of your precious time playing games and lurking on strangers social media profiles.

Turn off all the unnecessary notifications on your phone. The constant pings can be very distracting and will urge you to keep checking your phone. You don't really need a sound alert for anything other than calls or alarms. Turn off all other notifications. This way you will be less tempted to reply to texts instantly and engage in meaningless conversations. Turning these notifications off will help you to focus on your work better.

Stop using your phone when you are with someone. Communicate with the person who is in front of you. These days, you see people sitting across from each other at restaurants with their heads in their phones. They are either clicking pictures of things or texting someone else. What is the point of sharing a meal with someone if you don't even pay attention to them? Constantly using smartphones can have a very negative impact on your real relationships with people. Many young people these days have no idea how to talk to people in person, remember any messages and missed calls you receive will still be there later on for you to reply to or call back when you are free.

Use labels to compartmentalize the applications on your phone. Create folders for different categories. Make tags that will tell you that certain apps are productive while the others are a waste of time. This will deter you from constantly using apps in the latter folder. You need to use small tricks like this to train yourself and get out of the bad habits you have formed over the years.

When you stop using your smartphone as much as you do now, you will learn how to make real use of it. It will help in reducing your bad habits on the phone and instead learn how to use it for your benefit. Don't use the phone to stalk someone's social media. Use it for keeping track of all your meetings and work during the day.

Being a minimalist with your smartphone will help you in so many different ways. First of all, reducing usage of social media will improve your mental health which should always be a priority. You will stop wasting time on pointless apps on your phone and spend it being more productive in real life. You will improve your communication with the people you spend time with and really connect with them. It will also help you in saving a ton of money that you usually spend every time you switch from one phone to another. Reducing your smartphone usage will help in increasing your awareness of the world around you. You will learn to be more present and live better.

Minimalism will help you in giving importance to the things that really matter in your life. A smartphone is just a gadget meant for your convenience. It should not be something that has such a negative impact on your life as it currently does. Use it for your benefit and reduce the amount of time that you waste on it. You can see how minimalism will help you in improving even the smallest aspects of your life.

Physical and mental overhaul

This is a little off the topic of minimalism but I thought since you are working on improving the material aspect of your life that maybe we can now spend a few minutes talking about how to improve the physical and mental side of your life so this is a little bonus chapter for you.

The amount of people suffering from Mental illness is something that is growing every single year and although we hear about mental health at the severe end of the spectrum there are millions of people who suffer from smaller cases of anxiety and depression due to the normal everyday stresses of life and as don't do anything to try combat this and instead chose to live this way day in and day out.

I myself was one of those people, I still am to an extent but I want to talk to you about something I implemented into my life a couple years back that has helped in reducing my periods of anxiety.

That thing is called gratitude. You see I used to be a person who always had something to complain about. Everything that happened in life I would always take the negative point of view on, I would always assume the negative outcome would occur in every situation. I was a "why me", "this always happens to me" person. This would cause anxiety, stress and anger on a regular basis and then every now and then it would cause a bout of depression.

I knew I had to change as my life was passing me by year by year and now that I have 3 kids I didn't want them to adopt my negative attitude, also if I kept this up I was going to end up a pretty miserable older person later in life if I got there at all.

I started watching YouTube videos and reading up on gratitude, lots of celebrities and successful business people always speak about the law of attraction and action. What this means is that whatever you focus on is what you will attract in your life. If your grateful for things then you will attract more things to be grateful for but if you complain then you will end up having more negative situations pop up for you to complain about.

Now having said that I have a bit of an exercise for you that I know you can benefit from doing everyday, it will take literally 5 minutes out of your day every morning and will start your day out on a positive note no matter how grumpy you were about getting up early and having to go to work.

I want you to buy yourself a notebook, yea that's right after you have read an entire book on getting rid of your stuff I want you to go and buy something else. This note book will be your gratitude journal and every morning before the normally daily stresses of life such as getting the kids up and to school and taking yourself off to work I want you to write down 10 things you are grateful for. It can be anything at all and you really shouldn't have to think to hard as believe me there are plenty. Things like the fact you woke up this morning is one, not everyone had that luxury this morning, it could be the warm bed you slept in or the breakfast you are about to have, there are millions of homeless people out there that would love to be in that situation. The kiss goodnight you got from your son or daughter before bed last night, appreciate that because I'm telling you the time is coming when that will be "un cool" for your child to do.

Write 10 things down every day and refer back to it throughout the day when the stresses of life get a hold of you. You will find doing this every day will slowly get rid of that negative energy and replace it with positive vibes that will attract more positive outcomes in your life.

It's impossible to be angry when you are grateful, they are two opposite emotions so they can't co-exist at any one moment in time and you have the choice on which one you want to feel. It's completely in your control.

Now for your physical health, to stay at your peak physical condition there are 4 things you need to get on top of and they are

1. sleep
2. nutrition
3. activity
4. stress

We will start with sleep, I want you to ask yourself a couple questions,

1. Do I feel like you get enough sleep every night?
2. When was the last time I woke up feeling refreshed?
3. How much energy do i have on a daily basis?

A lot of people say exercise and nutrition are the 2 most important factors in peak physical health but in my opinion sleep overrides exercise. Our bodies recover while we sleep not just from exercise but from all other activities and aspects of life. You take sleep out and we become lethargic both physically and mentally. Our ability to handle stress decreases, our patience wears thin and we age faster.

The optimal amount of sleep we get told to have is 8 hours a night if you have less than this on a consistent basis or even more than this it will absolutely affect your life in a negative way. Obviously their are many different factors that can get in the way of us getting these 8 hours a night and steps must be put in place to ensure we fit them in. This can require discipline like going to bed an hour earlier than you normally do. Make a conscious effort to increase or even decrease your sleep as required.

The next thing is nutrition and this is one that I would say 9 out of 10 people get wrong. The old saying goes you are what you eat and if you fill your body up with sugar and deep fried foods your body will not run at its optimum. One quick improvement you can make which will have an instant effect is cutting out soda and adding in water. You will be amazed at how much sugar is in soda and because it's not food people don't always account for the calories that come in this way.

Even if this is th only change you make it will have a positive impact beyond belief.

The next thing is to add a serving of vegetables with every meal. Even if you continue to eat those deep fried foods for every meal if you add a serving of vegetables to that you will improve your health 100x, this doesn't have to be an all or nothing thing. From then you can look at the way you have your protein source, do you have fried chicken or do you grill some chicken breast on the BBQ? Do you trim the fat off your steak? All of these little things help and it doesn't have to be done at once. You can start by cutting your soda intake slightly and Increasing your water intake slightly and then go from there. The energy you will get from fixing your diet and sleeping pattern up will amaze you and you will wonder why you didn't start sooner.

After this I would then look at exercise. Now when I say exercise I don't mean you have to become a gym junkie and pump iron 6 days a week, it could be something as simple as ac30 minute walk 3 times a week. You could set aside time to do this or you could look to fit this in to your normal daily routine like getting off the bus 1 stop earlier and walking the rest of the way to work or you could take the stairs instead of the elevator through out the day.

In addition to this you could make it part of your routine to do 20 push-ups, 20 bodyweight squats, 20 sit-ups, 20 lunges every morning and evening. It will seriously take up 5-20 minutes depending on your current strength level and will give you amazing benefits not just physically but mentally. Seeing your strength go up as the weeks go by is a pretty cool thing as well and will give you an injection of confidence that you don't get from many other things.

The last part of the big 4 is stress levels. This once can be a tough one to break as some people just naturally stress over anything no matter how insignificant it can appear to people on the outside looking in. I am one of those people, I will stress over things that haven't happened and may not ever happen so it was something I had to get a hold of as it began to cause me a lot of anxiety day in and day out.

Some thing I do to help me conquer this is first to practice deep breathing. If you are in a situation where you can feel yourself getting stressed and anxious you need to stop whatever your doing and sit on a chair if your not already. Sit up with your shoulders back chest up and back straight. Begin by taking a big deep breath in and then breath out nice and slowly. Repeat this 3 or 4 times, this will bring your heart rate down, then go ahead and tell yourself that what ever it is that's stressing you out is not that bad, it's not the end of the world. What ever it is will be short lived, it will come to an end and if it's something you can't change right there in that moment then stressing out is not going to change anything except your mental state so why do it?

Another thing you can do it is to stretch. This is not necessarily something you can do at the specific time you feel stressed out but it's something you can do at night after a stressful day to help relieve tension in your body. It also relaxes you mentally and is good for you physically. When stretching remember to keep your breathing nice and controlled and you could also put some soft calming music on in the background.

Th last thing I do is to basically distract yourself from the specific issue that's causing you stress. If you are home you could put on your favorite tv show, what I like to do is search YouTube for a few minutes normally for things that will make me laugh to lighten the mood. You will be surprised at how a quick laugh can over shadow a negative moment and help reinforce the fact that whatever is worrying you is really not that bad.

Conclusion

Thank you once again for choosing this book.

Creating the minimalist look might sound simple but it is anything but that. It takes great skill and imaginative flair to create a beautiful room with the minimum of furniture, fixtures, and fittings. Each element of the room has to be carefully thought about in order to create the desired effect. It also takes self-discipline to keep it clear and free of clutter.

The idea is to create a beautiful room that has a fresh appeal, that is relaxing, inviting, functional and practical and that still carries an air of elegance and sophistication. If you get it right, it can be a welcome haven to come home to after a busy and chaotic work schedule, a place where you can truly relax and enjoy the ambiance of a stress-free and uncluttered space

Reference

The Minimalists. (2019). Retrieved from https://www.theminimalists.com/

becker, j., Becker, j., Becker, j., Becker, j., & Becker, j. (2019). Becoming Minimalist. Retrieved from http://www.becomingminimalist.com/

Home Ideas - Decorating and DIY Advice for the Home. (2019). Retrieved from https://www.goodhousekeeping.com/home/

Tiny House Archives - Tiny House Giant Journey. (2019). Retrieved from https://tinyhousegiantjourney.com/category/lifestyle/

Vesterfelt, A., Wise, C., Vesterfelt, A., Vesterfelt, A., Benedek, L., & Vesterfelt, A. et al. (2019). A Lighter, Simpler, More Beautiful Holiday. Retrieved from https://www.becomingminimalist.com/simpler-holiday/

Stewart, A., Stewart, A., Stewart, A., Stewart, A., Stewart, A., & Stewart, A. et al. (2019). Budget and the Bees - Buzz-worthy life tips for busy bees. Retrieved from https://budgetandthebees.com/

Minimalist Homes. (2019). Retrieved from http://www.minimalisthomes.com/

www.ingramcontent.com/pod-product-compliance
Lightning Source LLC
Chambersburg PA
CBHW032045290426
44110CB00012B/960